7 STEPS TO BONDING WITH YOUR STEPCHILD

7 STEPS TO BONDING WITH YOUR STEPCHILD

Suzen J. Ziegahn, Ph.D.

ST. MARTIN'S GRIFFIN
NEW YORK

www.stmartins.com

Library of Congress Cataloging-in-Publication Data

Ziegahn, Suzen J.
7 steps to bonding with your stepchild / Suzen J. Ziegahn.—1st ed.
p. cm
ISBN 0-312-25365-6
1. Stepchildren. 2. Stepparents. 3. Parent and child. 4. Child rearing.
I. Title: Seven steps to bonding with your stepchild. II. Title.

HQ777.7 .Z54 2001
306.874—dc21   00-045856

First Edition: March 2001

10 9 8 7 6 5 4 3 2 1

To my partner
and best friend, Tim Gapen,
without whose continued
encouragement, this book
would not have been possible

Contents

Introduction

Daydreaming. That's what I used to do when things weren't going well in my stepfamily. Daydreaming took me away from the day-to-day struggles, conflicts, and disappointments. I daydreamed about a tropical island with clear blue water and palm trees. To me, this was paradise, and that's where I wanted to be when stepfamily problems surfaced.

But, back in reality, I kept thinking about what I could do to make my stepfamily more workable—and that's how I came to write this book. All of the information that I felt would be helpful to a stepparent and stepfamily is compiled in 7 *Steps to Bonding with Your Stepchild*. And it's here to help you, too.

It seemed so simple. I needed to develop a relationship with my stepchildren. That would make everything better, right? They would see me as a person, a real person. And, of course, the key to this new family was my partner—the children's father. He could influence their attitudes toward me, couldn't he?

Simple ideas, yes. But complicated paths to get there? You bet. And although you will certainly need your spouse's support, bonding with your stepchild will demand serious effort, energy, and compassion from you. As you read through 7 *Steps to Bonding with Your Stepchild*, you may discover the work that's required to make this work. But keep *your* paradise in front of you, as the goal you are working toward, because gradually and eventually your stepfamily *can* become your paradise. After all, isn't paradise the place where you feel safe, where you want to feel your best? You can find it in your own stepfamily.

7 STEPS TO BONDING WITH YOUR STEPCHILD

STEP ONE

Recognizing Different Relationships

"When I married my husband, I knew, of course, that he had children. What I didn't know was that there would be multiple relationships going on in the family at the same time: one with me, a completely separate one between his kids and him, and another one between his kids and me."

I am always surprised at this statement when I hear it from an unsuspecting second wife and new stepmom. I shouldn't be; I felt the same way when I first entered the role myself. Why do we think that when we marry someone, especially with children, only one relationship will be operating in our marriage?

The answer is simple. When we marry the person we love, we want that person to think only of us. We want to be the most important and special person in our spouse's life. If I could wave a magic wand over each stepparent in the world and wish that to be true, I would. But it's just not going to happen in the stepfamily. Why? Because there are other distinct relationships operating simultaneously. Your relationship with your spouse is only one; your spouse and his children comprise the other; and there is also the big one—the one between your stepchildren and you. This creates a complex combination of people, personalities, roles, and rules operating at the same time.

The key is for each of these relationships to coexist within the stepfamily. Only when you acknowledge and respect each relationship will you achieve a balance of trust, love, and a happy home within your stepfamily. But first you need to recognize that distinct relationships exist in *each* stepfamily, and help your stepchild to understand this as well.

Defining Relationships that Already Exist in Your Stepfamily

Let's define the relationships within your stepfamily. The relationship between you and your partner is easy. You love each other and a relationship develops naturally. Another relationship exists between your spouse and his or her children. There are times when this one may be difficult for you to accept. This will depend on how you, as the stepparent, deal with certain givens in the stepfamily. First, it is a given that the stepchildren existed before your arrival into the family. Second, your spouse has some type of relationship with his children. Third, and most important, the stepchildren will be a part of your marriage, your stepfamily, and your life.

There is a third relationship created from the first two—the one you, the stepparent, have with your stepchildren. This relationship can be smooth or difficult, and it's mostly up to you as a stepparent in the approach you take with your stepchildren. It takes work and cooperation from both of you because instant love doesn't always develop automatically between stepparents and stepchildren. But this is not unusual. When you meet someone you might want to be friends with, a degree of work goes into the growth of that relationship. The stepparent-stepchild relationship is similar. The key difference is that the stepchild will *always* be there, whether or not a positive relationship unfolds. People we choose as friends may come and go, but we do not choose our stepchildren and they are there for the duration.

As a stepparent, it is to your advantage to develop a tolerable, hopefully positive, relationship with your stepchild as soon as possible. It will encourage the survival of your stepfamily—and your marriage because the relationship you have with your stepchild may redefine the relationship you have with your partner. How? By adding a new facet to an intimate relationship that would not normally exist between two adults without children.

RELATIONSHIP FACTORS

Stepfamily relationships are based on different factors, depending upon the reasons why each relationship developed. The relationship with your partner is based on personal selection, intimate love, and mutual respect. But the relationship with your stepchild is based on the fact that he or she is the child of the person you love. The concept is similar to the old adage "You can choose your friends but you cannot choose your family." Although you did choose your mate, you may not have necessarily wanted to become a stepparent. (This also applies to the children not having a choice in having you as a stepparent!)

The factors involved in the relationship between your spouse and her children are biological in nature, so don't even try to change it. This bond cannot be tampered with or taken lightly. If you decide to get in the middle of this one, I can only caution you to pick your battles carefully.

RELATIONSHIP FOUNDATIONS

Your relationships are also developed on different foundations. Hopefully the relationship between you and your spouse is based on a concrete foundation grounded in marriage. On the other hand, the relationship with your stepchild is built on a foundation that might be compared to eggshells. This relationship can crumble at any time and needs a great deal of work to build something strong and lasting. The foundation holding your spouse and his children together is as strong and powerful as the relationship between you and your spouse; these two strengths are different from one another and can coexist. It is essential that a stepparent know this, believe it, and respect it. Your spouse will not choose you over his child, so please do not expect him to. But, if he does, and you feel victorious about it, examine the reasons why and the morals behind it.

RELATIONSHIP GOALS AND ROUTINES

The relationship with your spouse might be enhanced by similar financial, social, or retirement goals. You may both want the same quality of life, and wish to possess the unique ability to thrive and grow in a stepfamily and maintain a longterm marriage. However, with your stepchild you might need to learn to live together by tolerating one another. Learn the key routines that your spouse and his children follow, honor those routines, and learn how to accept a stepchild into *your* life.

Learning to live with another person takes time. If you've ever had a roommate, there was undoubtedly an adjustment period. The same concept applies to a stepchild—at first it can be compared to having a roommate. This new roommate may have habits and routines that you are not crazy about, and your first instinct might be to change some of these habits. Let me caution you. Before you try to change anything, please take the time to observe, examine, and learn about the routines that bind your spouse and your stepchildren. If you suddenly start changing things, you may be treading into deep water and upsetting sensitive burial grounds that existed long before you arrived on the scene.

Lacy knew that Tony spent Tuesday evenings having dinner with his children and that this routine had been going on for five years. Once Lacy and Tony were married, Lacy told the children that they would not be having dinner on Tuesdays together any longer because that was her only evening alone with Tony. Lacy, of course, had underestimated the meaning of the Tuesday dinners for Tony and his children. Tony was upset, the children were upset, and Lacy learned quickly that independent decision-making is not workable in a stepfamily. Everyone must be considered in a decision and compromise is paramount.

One way to foster the relationship between you and your step-child is to learn to accept her on whatever level you can. Ignoring or denying this concept will hurt any chances of a relationship with your stepchild, and harm the one with your spouse. Whether you want limited contact with your stepchild or you want to fully embrace her in your life, you must accept your stepchild in some way. Otherwise, your relationship will be harmed because your spouse will interpret this as you not want-ing to include his children in your marriage and into your life as a family. Your spouse will resent you because he thought he married someone that wanted to be part of *his* family, which includes his children.

How Are These Relationships Intertwined?

Relationships in the stepfamily are intricately intertwined. As a stepparent, you may not notice this correlation immediately, but I assure you that at some point in your stepparent experi-ence, you will. For example, think of areas in your life that you have needed to balance, prior to your stepfamily experience, such as your professional life and personal life. Now think of how these two important factors in your life interconnect and affect one another. You might want your work hours to accom-modate your home life, or you might worry about how your in-come affects the quality of your life outside of work. These issues are incredibly important, and the relationships within your stepfamily should be equally important. In fact, these relationships should be a priority in your life. Why? Because in just about everything you do in your stepfamily, these relationships will connect, intersect, and bounce off of each other. Take, for example, scheduled weekend visits. There is probably a routine set up between your spouse and her ex-spouse for weekend visits with their children. The slightest change in this schedule affects every relationship in your stepfamily, whoever initiates it. Why? Because your stepfamily life and your individual life are generally planned around this routine. It is imperative that communication be open between all members of the stepfamily to create a balance and the least disruption possible. Your actions will affect these relationships, and your communication will affect them as well.

The link between the relationships that keeps them intricately intertwined is your spouse, the biological parent, who will also be there for the duration of your marriage and stepfamily. Your spouse will continually look at both relationships when making a decision that affects the household because she loves you *and* her child. You want your opinion recognized, and so does your stepchild. Often it's easier for us to disregard our stepchild's opinion. For example, you may feel that the stepchild's opinion reflects his biological parent's views or vice versa. Or perhaps you simply don't see why your stepchild's opinion is important. For years, Sally disregarded her stepchild's opinion, feeling it would make no difference or have any affect on her own decision-making in the family. Her husband, Tom, became resentful, wanting to defend the child against this continual unfairness, and the relationship deteriorated into divorce. In any event, if you want your stepfamily to move forward as a unit, these relationships must connect.

The Relationships Must Be Kept Separate

Just as the relationships must interconnect, they must also be kept purposely and carefully separate. I know this sounds confusing, but let me explain the need for this paradox, and how it can benefit you as a stepparent.

The relationships in your stepfamily are structurally different. You and your partner have an intimate love and passion for each other and want to be physically close. By the nature of those elements, you want to share the events of your days, plans for the future, and your goals and dreams. The relationship your partner has with his children is unconditional. He will also want to spend time with his children, be physically close to them, and share their days, their goals, and their dreams. Try not to feel neglected or threatened by this relationship.

Brooke came in for counseling feeling alienated in her marriage to Ben. Recently Ben had said that he needed to know that his children were in their bedrooms upstairs in order to feel comfortable. This made her feel uneasy because she wanted Ben to include her in this statement. Brooke felt that Ben had this need to be close to his children that excluded her presence. She wanted Ben to feel secure knowing that *she* was near, and she had thought Ben felt this way ever since they met. But when

Brooke found out instead that Ben felt that security only with his children's presence, she immediately felt alienated.

In working with Brooke, it became clear that she had fallen into a common pattern of many stepparents—feeling that the stepchildren substitute or replace them as stepparents. Sometimes we feel that our spouse's children are more important to them. Doesn't this sound like something a stepchild would feel? It continually occurs to me that we, as adults, can have the same insecurities about being replaced that a child has. In this particular situation, Brooke discovered that Ben's feelings for his children's presence in the house were perfectly natural—something she understood all along—but when Ben vocalized this, it took her off guard and struck an insecure cord. Feeling hurt and acting on impulse, Brooke chose not to discuss this with Ben, and it festered and swelled to the point where it caused a rift between them. Brooke needed help to understand how she sometimes reacts to comments, and how she can control and change her way of receiving information and responding to it.

Structurally, the relationship that you have with your stepchildren may have some physical distance to it. You may try not to live in the same areas of the house, for example. By nature of this, you may not even think about sharing your days, plans for the future, and certainly not your goals and dreams. In other words, it takes work to begin to even think about how this relationship with your stepchild will be structured, and how that structure will fit into the other two relationships within the stepfamily.

Managing These Relationships Simultaneously

The difficult part is managing all of these relationships at once. Sounds impossible. Sounds like a lot of work. Impossible—no. A lot of work—yes. But if the relationships need to be separate, why do we need to manage them simultaneously? Why can't we just function in each relationship separately at different times? Because we would be on the same train going in different directions; we would be heading in the same direction initially but suddenly end up in two completely different places. The key is to manage the relationships so that we are on the same train with the same destination. How? The best way is by knowing our boundaries.

Sheridan and Colton were married just a year when their stepfamily fell apart—literally. Sheridan came in to see me after she had moved out of the stepfamily home. Sheridan admitted that, in the stepfamily, she functioned independently of Colton and his children. When she made weekend plans for the two of them she did not include the children. So, Colton was often left in an uncomfortable spot with his ex-wife because she had already made plans for the kids' weekend with their father. When Colton wanted to discuss the children, Sheridan would often criticize anything and everything about them, offering no positives to show that she shared his feelings of pride for his children. Sheridan did not respect her boundaries with the children's mother or with Colton's decisions and feelings about his children. It didn't take Colton long to tire of Sheridan's resistance to his children, and they soon parted, now needing intensive work to reconcile their marriage and stepfamily.

BOUNDARIES, BOUNDARIES, BOUNDARIES...

You've heard people talk about boundaries, but why are they so important? Have you ever had someone walk in on a private conversation you were having on the telephone? Or have you been interrupted while you were doing something personal? Better yet, have you ever walked in on something that you felt embarrassed about later and wished you had thought about first? This is why boundaries are important—so that we are not irritated by an interruption and we respect others in similar situations.

Boundaries are important in traditional families but keenly significant in the stepfamily. Why? Because of unconditional love. We respect our parents and our siblings, and if we happen to step across a boundary with them, there is still a binding love present. But when you cross a stepchild's boundary uninvited, he is not likely to forget it. The incident becomes ammunition for a good case against your presence in the family. This doesn't mean stepchildren are bad people. They just may not have wanted you around anyway, and when you infringe on their personal space, you help them confirm that feeling. So, make an effort to *learn the boundaries* between you and your stepchild, as well as how much your spouse wants you to be involved in her relationship with her child; better yet, help set them.

■ *Determining Boundaries*

Ideally, boundaries should be determined by the adults and the child together, and often they will depend upon the child's age. You and your spouse should have this discussion very shortly after you move in together. In any cohabitation situation between two people, an adjustment period exists regarding toothpaste squeezings and toilet-paper-roll positions. The same issues will occur with the stepchild and stepparent.

Gradually the issues will become more complicated and sticky and you will need to talk about them. Why? Because if you haven't talked about and agreed upon where to take off dirty shoes when you come in from outside, how will you deal with your teenage stepdaughter bringing home six friends looking for pizza and snacks during your book-reading group? Unless you are all going to eat pizza and read books together like one big happy family, I suggest you address boundaries, from the simple everyday issues to the more complicated ones that *will* arise. And please include your spouse in the discussions about boundary setting. Remember, boundaries may already exist between your spouse and his child. You will want to integrate those already-present boundaries with the new ones. Why? Your stepchild is already comfortable with them. Changing boundaries that have already been set might give your stepchild an opportunity to resent you. And you don't want—or need—that.

Boundaries are more important for older children. If your stepchild is younger than ten years old, the boundaries might focus more on everyday routines. For example, if you and your spouse are having a conversation, your stepchild should wait until you are finished before interrupting, and the same applies to you if your spouse and his child are conversing. As the children grow older, more difficult issues will present themselves. At this time, boundaries will need to be set with all members of your stepfamily present.

■ *Changing Boundaries*

Once boundaries have been established and agreed to by all stepfamily members, it is imperative that no one person change the rules without notifying other family members. It is especially important that the biological family members not change the rules in midstream without telling you, the stepparent. You need to make this clear to your stepfamily members. Sometimes biological family members change a routine, agree to the change, and just start doing it. They might forget to tell you, and even though it might be an innocent gesture on their part, it can cause much emotional damage to the stepfamily relationship. If the rest of the family make decisions without you, it sends a message that you are not considered a strong, active member of the stepfamily—and frankly, it can hurt your feelings and make you feel like an outsider all over again. Hurt feelings cause internal damage, particularly hurt feelings that are not addressed, discussed, shared, and resolved regardless of the outcome.

Greg and Brenda had been married six years when an issue came up that surprised Brenda. Greg's children, Timothy and Victoria, were in their midteens when, one day, Brenda discovered through a conversation with her stepdaughter that Greg discussed their financial situation with his children. Brenda's red flag went up immediately; although she cared for Timothy and Victoria, she wanted certain aspects of her relationship with Greg to remain separate from the children. One of these areas was their financial future. Brenda had been raised in a family where money was discussed between the parents and did not include the children. Greg felt that he wanted to discuss their financial situation with his children so that Timothy and Victoria could learn more about how to manage money and handle it in a family situation.

This situation caused much anxiety for Brenda. Not only did she not want to share their finances, she also felt that Greg was completely ignoring her perspective. Greg and Brenda had never even reached the point of discussing each side thoroughly because both of them had become angry at the beginning and could not get past the initial suggestion of the idea.

Once Greg and Brenda were both able to discuss their position on the issue, they could then understand what they needed to do. It was important to Greg that Timothy and Victoria learn about money matters. It was equally important to Brenda that their financial situation remain their own private concern. Once they were able to vocalize their feelings to each other, they then compromised on this issue. Brenda agreed that as they entered adulthood, Greg's children could be included in some of their conversations in order to help guide and teach them. Greg also understood that he could teach the children about money matters in different ways, without sharing personal information that could seriously harm the intimacy of his relationship with Brenda; something he clearly did not wish to risk. Both agreed to future conversations about which issues were open to discussion with the children and which issues were clearly off limits.

This example reveals why it is important to identify and maintain boundaries. Each person in the relationship brings his or her own ideas about how to do things—including raising children/stepchildren. Many times couples mistakenly assume that their partner feels the *same* way about certain issues. Or they believe that their partner *will* agree simply out of love. Keeping your boundaries intact and sharing issues that are unique to only you and your partner, allows you to maintain a degree of control and predictability in your relationship.

The relationship between you and your spouse can suffer damage without discussion, agreement, and compromise.

Keep Your Relationship with Your Partner Special and Separate

You have waited for this relationship and have finally found the person that you want to be with for the rest of your life. It is wonderful, it is special, it is a priority in your life—keep it that way! In a stepfamily, it can be difficult to remember why your relationship with your spouse is special—or why you wanted to be in this relationship in the first place! Try this exercise. Take a few minutes, right now, and jot down the reasons why you love your spouse, and what drew you to him or her initially. Then, review the list—it may trigger a romantic memory or a humorous incident that happened between the two of you. This is a nice way of reminding yourself of how much you care about your spouse and why. Our busy lives can sometimes get in the way of remembering the truly loving moments in our lives. Keep the list handy. You may need to review it from time to time, when the going might get rough in the stepfamily.

Now think about what you have done lately to keep your relationship with your partner special and separate. If you are drawing a blank, you may need to work at this. Try to remember the last time you had a romantic look or wink at each other, went out for a special dinner for just the two of you, or experienced whatever kind of intimate moment that, to you and your spouse, keeps the relationship special. People experience love in different ways. The touch of a hand, the wink of an eye, or a kind word to each other reminds you of your love and respect for one another. As you work and get involved in activities during the week, it's easy to forget these things and perhaps take your partner for granted. This can be dangerous to any relationship, but with the added pressures in a stepfamily, it can be disastrous. It is paramount that you make time for each other, in whatever way works for you. If you can set aside one evening a week for just you and your spouse, great. If you feel you can't afford that kind of time, make a date to do something together once a week for a couple of hours, but try not to go any longer than that.

Think of creative ways to keep your relationship special. Let your mind wander and try not to limit yourself. Include things like cruising down the Amazon, laying on the beach of a not-so-inhabited island, or going to your favorite picnic spot. Once you have finished, go back and prioritize the list of ideas according to what is realistic given your lifestyle and economic situation. Based on how comfortable you feel with your ideas, share them with your partner or fold the list and keep it where you can retrieve it from time to time. This is a great way to share some intimate time with your partner, and perhaps develop and schedule a future activity together!

The Adult Relationship Must Be Respected

Along the lines of cherishing your intimate relationship, your stepchildren also need to respect the adult relationship. Why is this so important? Well, for one thing, your stepchildren need to see how much you love and respect their parent. It will earn you their respect, and if they feel that you love their parent, they will feel more secure with you as a member of the family. Stepchildren want the best for their parent. So, you should want to be the best.

It is also important for the stepchildren to know that the adult relationship is important, because you are a model for these children. Whether your stepchildren marry and have biological children or find themselves in a stepfamily, they will remember how you, as a stepparent, handled it. If you can be a good model, you can reduce the tension in future families.

VIEWING RELATIONSHIPS AS TEMPORARY

Stepchildren tend to view their biological parents' relationships with others as temporary. This is partly because they don't want their parents to be in other permanent relationships. Some stepchildren feel threatened by these relationships because their parent's attention will now be directed at someone else. It is safer for stepchildren to think the adult relationship is temporary. It helps them to rationalize thoughts such as "Well, my dad isn't going to be with this person long anyway, so I don't have to do what she tells me." Sometimes when a stepchild's parent breaks up with another adult, it also gives the child the opportunity to say to themselves, "See, I knew my Mom loved me better."

Remember, children that come from a divorced family often feel these insecurities and find ways to hang on to their biological parents' love. So, if your stepchild feels that your marriage is temporary, this has nothing to do with you as a person—she's simply reacting to the situation. But human nature makes it difficult to accept this without taking it personally. Try to be aware of what your stepchild has gone through, to understand the origin of her feelings and, perhaps, comments.

A stepchild may also think that since you won't be around long anyway, he doesn't need to get to know you or make any effort to accommodate you. These are very common feelings among stepchildren and are often related to the fantasy about their parents getting back together that is discussed further in Chapter Three.

What should you do if your stepchild exhibits any of the above behaviors or comes right out and tells you that he feels you won't be around long? There are several ways that you can handle this, but first please give significant thought to your approach. Remember that your stepchild has a history and is functioning based on past experiences, either with his parents' other relationships, wanting his parents back together, or both. Therefore, the comment may not be meant as a direct hit to you personally, but be realistic about this; only you can judge how your stepchild really feels about you. Try not to react too quickly or with anger. Your goal is to get your stepchild to change his thinking about the "temporary status" of your marriage. In order to do that, the stepchild will need to invest time and energy in this relationship with you. Be aware, however, that your stepchild may have a fear of investing too much because you and his parent may divorce, just like his real parents did.

GIVING YOUR STEPCHILDREN A SENSE OF PERMANENCE

If stepchildren see that your relationship with their parent is solid, strong, *and* longterm, they think you are trustworthy. In my experience, if stepchildren feel confident that you are going to be their stepparent, they are more willing to work with you within the family unit.

But how can they be sure that you are going to be around? One surefire way is for their parent to talk with them about your long-term relationship. The words of a biological parent are close to gospel, and chances are the stepchildren will believe and trust what their parent tells them about your relationship. But ultimately, if the stepchildren see the strength and closeness in your relationship with their parent, you're in. One cautionary piece of advice; in my experience, stepchildren are also keenly aware when problems arise in your relationship with their parent. It's wise to recognize that disagreements should be discussed in private with your spouse, particularly if it is between the two of you.

A stepfamily experiencing difficulty with their relationships appeared at my door one day. This family consisted of Angela, the mother, Cameron, the stepfather, and Cole, the son. Angela and Cameron had been married for three years and had dated for nearly seven years prior to their marriage. Both agreed that they had a good marriage, but they also agreed that the one obstacle in their marriage seemed to be the way Cole viewed his mother and stepfather's relationship. Cole accepted Cameron's presence in the house, but he continually made comments about their relationship ending. Curious about this, I asked for specific examples.

Angela described Cole's remarks. She reported that Cole would say things such as, "Ya know, Mom, it's fine that Cameron goes to the beach with us on weekends and stuff, but when you aren't seeing him anymore, we can do this all by ourselves again—like we used to." Angela went on to say that when Cole made these remarks she would explain to him that she and Cameron were married and that Cameron wasn't planning on going anywhere. According to Angela, Cole would say, "Sure Mom," and walk away or continue with what he was doing.

Angela grew increasingly concerned with her son's behavior. After all, she and Cameron had been together for ten years now, and Cole still refused to accept Cameron as his stepfather or a permanent member of this stepfamily. We spent a good deal of time discussing how Cameron felt about this situation. Cameron felt mostly confused, frustrated by Cole's indifference, and sometimes felt as though maybe he *should* leave.

In the future times that we met together, we discussed Cole's history as a child, what happened to his father, where his father was now, and how Cole had dealt with the loss of his traditional family structure. As more information was revealed, we discovered that Cole had a friend who was in the same stepfamily situation. Cole's friend's parent, however, seemed to go through relationships quickly, and they never lasted very long. Cole was a sensitive, easily influenced child, and seemed to listen to everything this friend told him, such as, "Don't worry, Cameron won't last. Yeah, yeah, he's been around a long time, but stepparents never stick around and your Mom will move on to somebody else eventually." And, since his Mom and Dad had divorced, Cole didn't believe that there was any permanency to his mother and Cameron's marriage, either. Cole needed to be convinced that his mother and Cameron were planning a lifelong marriage.

First, we examined if Angela and Cameron had verbal arguments at home. As with any relationship, they had. We then discussed what types of things were said. It turned out that Cameron had said on occasion that he would leave if things didn't get better, and Angela would respond saying, "Fine, go." Cole would overhear this sometimes, and it would only validate what his friend had told him. We talked about reducing the verbal altercations and changing the *way* Angela and Cameron argued, specifically using the method of listening and focusing on what the other is really saying, rather than simply blurting out angry responses. After some practice, this solved the problem to a degree.

We then addressed Cole's feelings about the permanency of marriage. This was a much more indepth issue to discuss, but by the end of Cole's and my individual time together, and continued stepfamily sessions, Cole had learned that marriage still means permanency, and that Angela and Cameron take their vows seriously and plan to be a stepfamily forever. Cole learned an important and valuable lesson about relationships, so that he, when an adult, can make choices in relationships for himself. If Angela and Cameron had not come in for help with this issue,

Cole might have leaped into adulthood thinking that relationships hold no permanency, which could have hurt his chances for intimacy and affected how he felt about trusting other people in the future. Of course, there is no way to predict how Cole's adult relationships might have turned out, but Angela, his mother, discussed her feelings of how pleased she was that Cole had this opportunity to explore this issue in his teenage years. It gave Angela a sense of peace about her son's future.

Build a Separate Relationship with Your Stepchild

Just as your stepchild needs to recognize that the adult relationship is important and special, so do you need to acknowledge a separate relationship with your stepchild. I have spoken to stepparents who believe that their stepchildren are lumped together with their spouse. These stepparents don't see their stepchildren as separate people with individual feelings, opinions, and lives. This may work when your stepchildren are young, but once they become teenagers moving rapidly into adulthood, it will be a shock to suddenly see them as separate human beings. They will probably start telling you how they think and feel, whether or not you are prepared. So, the sooner you create a separate relationship with your stepchild, the better.

WHAT KIND OF RELATIONSHIP DO YOU WANT TO HAVE WITH YOUR STEPCHILD?

As the adult, you clearly need to be the one who initiates the relationship between you and your stepchild. Two of the first issues to consider are how you feel about your stepchild and how you want your relationship to work together. For example, if you feel very close to her, then your relationship will undoubtedly be one of openness and sharing on a more frequent basis. You may feel comfortable discussing a variety of issues and participating in activities together.

If you don't feel as close to your stepchild, it will be more difficult to communicate. So, you may want to ask yourself some questions. Do I want to communicate with my stepchild? Why or why not? If I want to communicate with him, do I want to discuss personal issues or remain more on the surface, discussing only broad topics? How much information do I want to share about myself? My goal is for you to understand why it's important to do some initial homework on your own in thinking about the relationship you can have with your stepchild, and, perhaps, give you some ideas on how to go about forming this bond.

HOW TO ENCOURAGE A STEPCHILD TO INVEST TIME AND ENERGY INTO A RELATIONSHIP WITH YOU

There are several ways stepchildren can develop a relationship with you. However, if they know they are doing this, it probably won't work as well. Try to get them involved through activities that they enjoy or, better yet, are their idea.

Find out about your stepchild's hobbies and interests. Ask him directly, but if you keep getting the "I don't know" answer, ask your partner for help. Generally, parents are a wealth of knowledge about their children and love to talk about them. So here's your chance—talk to your partner, and by showing this level of interest in her child, you will gain points that will increase bonding in your own relationship! After you have gathered information on what your stepchild likes to do, give some thought to planning an activity with him. This doesn't have to be a mega outing; it can be a simple pastime that you can enjoy together. If your stepchild likes to read, find out what types of books he likes and suggest a trip to the bookstore, or have him bring you a book from the library. But before you suggest this, it might be a good idea to approach him gradually and begin talking about how much you like reading and the kinds of books you like to read.

I worked with a stepparent who discovered, through this method, that she had a passion for the identical type of nonfiction reading that her stepdaughter did—and she found this out after living with her stepdaughter for five years! I suggested they work together on a project, finding various books on the subjects they both enjoyed and sharing books back and forth. This opened an opportunity for the stepmom to spend time with her stepdaughter, sharing a mutual interest that was unique to them. What a terrific basis for creating a lifelong shared passion and bond. The stepdaughter invested time and energy into getting to know her stepmom, without consciously realizing she was doing it!

Another way to encourage a stepchild to invest time in you is for you to get to know your stepchild's friends. Kids tend to be influenced by their friends' opinions, and if you relate to your stepchild's friends, there is a good chance your stepchild will look at you in a different way—a positive way. Great things can come from this method. You will get to know your stepchild and her friends better, discovering what they like, what they don't like, and, possibly, what's going on in their lives. Stepchildren may remain guarded at first, but eventually they will open up as they feel more comfortable. Telling you what is happening in their life is a major coup. Through this method, you may also get to know the parents of your stepchild's friends, who may even be stepparents themselves. Sharing information with other stepparents can offer you valuable advice *and* enable you to help another stepparent's survival.

Try one or more of the ideas presented or create one of your own. Your stepchild's response will be determined partially by *your* openness to it. You can help your stepchild get to know you and bond with you.

THE DIFFERENCE BETWEEN BEING A FRIEND AND BEING A PARENT

One of the best ways to build a rapport with your stepchild is to balance being a friend with being the new parent. As you may be thinking, there is an incredibly fine line between the two roles. If you act only as a parent, you may create a wall between you and your stepchild; he will see you only as an authority figure and resist any efforts on your part to socialize with him. But how do you be a parent and a friend? Well, interestingly, this is easier to accomplish in the stepparent role.

As a stepparent, you will participate in raising your stepchildren, and the stepchildren need to recognize this. But you also have an opportunity to be a companion, mentor, and friend to your stepchildren outside of the parenting role. How? Even though you are an additional parent to them, you are still different from their biological parents. And when children need to confide in someone, often they will not confide in their parents, for any number of reasons. They see their parents as just that— their parents, and fail to see individual character qualities that other people see. For example, your own father or mother may be a wonderful listener, but would you have realized that when you were growing up? Probably not.

Your stepchildren see you as an adult, outside of the parental definition of adults, which to children doesn't exist (parents are not adults, they are parents!). If you approach your stepchildren correctly, you can be both the disciplinarian/parent and someone they respect enough to confide in and share important details of their lives with. So, put on your best diplomatic face, and be stepchild-friendly. This will increase the chance of a successful stepparent-stepchild relationship. Plus, there is always the possibility that your stepchild likes you (good for you), admires you, and would like to be friends with you. Getting your stepchild to like you as a person, a separate individual from his biological parent, will allow your stepchild to see your strengths and weaknesses. It will encourage your stepchild to make conscious choices about relationships with other adults he chooses to spend time with, and chooses as a mentor for his own life.

As you now know, recognizing the relationships that exist in your stepfamily is really vital to the survival of your family, and important to the success of the relationship with your spouse.

2

Understand Your Partner's View

"I just don't know what's wrong with John. When we first started dating he was wonderful to me. Now, after just six months of marriage, he is distant and moody. I thought this marriage was going to be different."

Sound familiar? Yes, unfortunately, these statements reflect the thoughts of those of us who find ourselves in a second marriage to someone we felt would be different—he or she would be romantic and loving, would listen, and would genuinely care about our own thoughts and feelings. The great part is that the new man or woman in your life *does* care about your thoughts and feelings. The problem is that you may not understand why your spouse is unable to express it. People show their feelings in many different ways, but life has a way of placing obstacles in our path to showing our loved ones how we really feel.

Think of your own family and how you grew up within that

family. If it was a traditional family, think of the many ups and downs that occurred over a period of time—adding children to the family, financial stressors, perhaps in-law pressure. All of these factors, plus the ones you may have additionally experienced in your own family, contribute to blocking your attempts to show affection toward those you love. In thinking about the stressors in a traditional family, add the pressures unique to stepfamilies, and this will help explain why the new partner in your life may be experiencing difficulty and why he appears distant at times.

The Influence of Previous Relationships

One stressor in a stepfamily situation is the life carried over into the new marriage from the previous relationship. If you feel that your new partner is free and clear of any past experiences, particularly negative experiences, you're lucky. Chances are, this is not the case, however, and eventually the leftover stuff will resurface. It's likely that you have come into this new relationship bearing some scars inflicted long ago. This would be an excellent opportunity to examine that issue about yourself. Was a former relationship destructive in any way to you? Did you cause any destruction in your past relationships? Have you healed from any emotional upheaval that may have taken place in your life?

This chapter is about examining your partner's view of the stepfamily, but it is a great idea to look at yourself first. It will be difficult to understand where another person has traveled from if you are not sure of your own past journey and how it has affected who you are today. I urge you to be objective about yourself, be honest, and view this exercise as a necessary part of helping your stepfamily to succeed. If you find there are unresolved issues in your own emotional state, consider doing something about it. The more you know about yourself, the better stepparent and life partner you will become, and the more benefit you can be to your stepfamily.

Now let's look at your partner and where she has come from before this relationship. Perhaps your partner has been through a divorce or the death of a previous spouse. Whatever happened with your spouse, take the time now to think about that event in your partner's life. Has your spouse talked with you about it? Probably when you first met. Do you feel confident that you know what happened in that situation with your spouse? Do you feel that you have a handle on how your spouse felt about it— really felt about it? If the answer is yes, good. If you are uncertain, this is the time to explore your own knowledge of what happened to your spouse's last relationship.

Try this exercise. Write down briefly, in two or three sentences, a scenario of your understanding of how your partner came to be single. After you have completed the brief scenario, write down three emotions that you think your spouse may have felt as a result of that experience. Now prioritize the emotions that you jotted down, ranking them in order of importance. Review what you have written. Were you surprised at the emotions that you wrote down? Was this the first time that you realized that your partner may have experienced these emotions, or is still experiencing them? Now congratulate yourself. This is the first step toward searching for a deeper understanding of your partner's feelings, and the opening of a door into your future emotional sharing.

WHY YOU NEED TO KNOW HOW YOUR PARTNER FEELS ABOUT THE PAST

Your partner has been through emotional stages in past relationships that have not succeeded. We all know what those stages are—the initial happiness, confusion with a slow decline in communication and commitment, and the final resentment, dislike, perhaps even loathing that occurs when relationships dissolve. Living through a declining relationship can be a roller coaster ride of emotions, and it's difficult to know when to get off. Most of us sit tight and hang on until the end, which can be a humiliating experience if your spouse is leaving you.

But there is a whole set of emotions felt by the spouse who initiates the leaving. One of these emotions is guilt, and we tend to carry that for some time. Guilt is an interesting emotion, and people tend to behave peculiarly when they feel guilty. If left unresolved, this guilt and the other emotions we carry from previous relationships can go unchecked and easily slide right into our next relationship (although we may think we have resolved them). You think you have conquered these emotions, and then wham—one day you are in your new relationship and something comes out of your mouth that smacks of the feelings in that earlier relationship! Guess what? The emotion still lingers. This may also happen to your spouse.

It's likely that when some old emotions surface in our new relationship from our new spouse, we are quick to respond with anger. But just think, if we understood where those emotions were coming from, how much better we could respond and not make matters worse. It is imperative that we understand what stage our partner is in with regard to his past life. Has he resolved the issue that was bothering him? How was it resolved? Is he comparing you to his ex-spouse? If so, in what ways? What can you do to help your spouse move beyond this? These are all questions to ask yourself when a situation occurs during an argument or if something is said casually that, basically, rocks your world. If you can begin to understand where your partner is, particularly if he has work to do on resolving some issues, the better chance your relationship has of surviving. And to do some work in this department on your intimate relationship will reap precious rewards in building a successful step-family.

Another factor in helping to understand your partner's current perspective is knowing how long your partner has been without her ex-spouse. The more deep rooted these unresolved issues are, the tougher it will be to work through them. Although we are a society of highly intellectual beings, we sometimes cannot see ourselves and where we hurt, and particularly we can't see how we hurt others. I strongly recommend that you consider different methods for tackling this situation. Possible options are professional therapy and counseling, talking honestly between the two of you, or engaging in a discussion with a trusted parent, friend, or mentor. Whatever situation you decide works best for you, try not to wait too long. Time is important when you are trying to build a stable and strong stepfamily.

I worked with a couple who came in one day looking to find an answer to their gradual discontentment with each other. Neither Kelly nor Brock could specifically verbalize what was wrong. So, we began by "peeling away at the onion," folding back layers of their daily lives to try to pinpoint the root of the problem. It took several sessions together, as well as individual sessions with each of them, but they revealed an emotion that Brock felt when his ex-wife left him with his three children and lost all contact with them. This had occurred six years earlier.

Brock clearly felt abandoned. He was left with the parenting of three children, the care and maintenance of a house, and being the sole supporter for the family, not only financially but also emotionally. Brock, as many other people who have experienced this kind of situation, simply moved on with his life. He did not seek professional help or talk with anyone, really, about the situation. He just did what he needed to do to survive.

When Kelly entered the picture, Brock appeared to be together, "as if he had his life in control," Kelly stated. Once married, about three months into their relationship, Brock started picking at Kelly. She wasn't cleaning well enough; her clothing wasn't just right, and he even began criticizing her during conversations about her work. Kelly reacted angrily to this, often storming away and not trying to work it through later with Brock. This behavior and response escalated to the point where their marriage was suffering, and relationships in the stepfamily were also suffering because of the continued tension in the home.

With much discussion and probing, Brock finally admitted that he started feeling that if his first wife abandoned him, then Kelly could just as easily leave him, too. So, he rationalized, if he abandoned her first, through criticism and making her feel inferior, then when she left him, he would not be as devastated and hurt. Once the problem was identified, Brock worked first on dealing with the abandonment from the first marriage, and then on rebuilding the second marriage.

This is an example of what can occur when issues are left unresolved. More importantly, it illustrates how unprepared we can be in a second marriage if we are unsure of where our partner is in dealing with his previous life.

■ *Benefits to Understanding Your Partner's Position*

Now, just what are the benefits of understanding your partner's position? There are several. The first benefit will be an added closeness to your spouse. Think of how you feel when your partner agrees with you on something. It's a warm and intimate feeling, and, as a result, you feel more bonded with your partner. You will grant your partner the same gift when you demonstrate that you understand her point of view. An appreciative partner is a happy partner, and who better to be appreciated by than the person you love most in your life?

Another benefit is to your stepfamily. Understanding your partner's view can be a building block to a stepfamily based on love, understanding, honesty, and trust. If you know and understand your partner's view, you will be able to merge this view with your own much more deliberately, clearly, and successfully.

33

ᴴefit personally from accepting your partner's view.
..passion will engender a respect from your partner that
...ıll probably last a lifetime. Remember that it is difficult for
anyone to confront painful issues, particularly from the past. By
understanding your partner's view, you will provide him with a
sense of relief about his new life in the stepfamily—and with
you, the new stepparent—that he could not give himself.

Finally, your stepchild will benefit. By acknowledging your
partner's view, you will begin to understand your stepchild's position in all of this. Children want to sympathize with their parents. In a divorce or death, the children will be more inclined
to sympathize with individual parents when they see them strug-
gling. By showing your stepchild that you, too, sympathize with
her parent, the stepchild can trust that your feelings for her
parent are genuine. Trusting you is such an important thing for
a stepchild. If your stepchild *trusts* that you care about her parent, this will create and/or strengthen a bond with your stepchild
that will be difficult to tear down—ever. A stepchild needs to
feel trust for her stepparent. Why? Because she trusts her biological parents unconditionally. If her parent chooses a partner,
an outsider, the stepchild's first test will be to see if she can
trust you. Why? Because she cannot bear to see her parent hurt
again. If your stepchild feels she cannot trust you, she may look
for ways to discredit you to your spouse, placing you in an immediately defensive position between your spouse and your stepchild, a place you probably don't want to be.

Remember that your actions, conversations, and behaviors
speak to your stepchildren. Show them that you care for and

understand their parent. Your stepchildren will interpret this as love, and loving their parent is a great step toward building a successful bond with your stepchildren. It is much easier to accept an "outsider" if the outsider can express love. Also, if your stepchildren see that you love their parent, often they will believe that you are capable of loving them, too. Why? Because stepchildren view themselves as a package with their parent—generally they do not see themselves as separate and independent parcels. They go where their parent does—and if that means into the same house as you, then you take the whole package, including them. In reality, stepchildren are both part of the package and a separate parcel—but for now, that's for the stepparent to know, understand, and accept.

Recognize Your Partner's View Toward the Effect of the Loss of One Parent on the Children

Knowing your partner's feelings about the loss of his previous partner and the surrounding circumstances is really only one part of the puzzle. The children are undoubtedly impacted by the loss or separation from their other parent, and the effects of this loss may not be obvious enough to deal with directly. The children may be experiencing a variety of emotions due to being without both parents together. These emotions can range from sadness, grief, numbness, and helplessness to anger, hostility, and blaming. It is important to recognize that one or more of these emotions may be operating within your stepchildren. The intensity will depend upon how recently their parents began to live apart. Examine the situation for a moment. How long have their parents been apart? Have your stepchildren displayed any of the above emotions when discussing their other parent? Or perhaps another emotion not mentioned? Write down your impressions of how you think your stepchildren feel about the loss of their other parent, and keep this written information for future review. If you have not thought about this issue before, I would encourage you to begin observing your stepchildren during conversations about their other parent, or noting how they react if the other parent is brought up briefly. You can "see" a lot about your stepchildren if you observe their body language and really "hear" what they are saying.

As important as it is for you to have an idea about how your stepchildren feel about losing their other parent, magnify that many times to understand how your partner feels about what her children are going through because of the divorce, or whatever situation separated them from the other parent. Your partner may not readily want to discuss this issue, feeling that you, as the stepparent, may not understand. Be prepared for that. I encourage you to probe this area to understand very clearly what your partner knows and is feeling toward the children. Is she sensitive to the children's feelings about their other parent? Is your partner in a protective mode regarding this issue with her children? Is she protective to the point of feeling that she needs to protect her children even from you? This can hurt, I know, but you must make the effort to try to understand how sensitive this issue may be for your partner, and for your stepchildren. You may say something about the other parent that could be misinterpreted—a perfectly innocent statement on your part but, given the degree of sensitivity within your stepfamily, words can be taken the wrong way.

HOW YOUR PARTNER'S ATTITUDE AFFECTS YOUR RELATIONSHIP WITH THE CHILDREN

Your partner's view can interfere with your relationship with your stepchildren in two ways. First, if your partner feels that his children need to be protected from another adult's influence, it can interfere with your partnering on many issues, including parenting the children together. For example, let's say you feel the need to correct your stepchild's behavior on picking up after herself. Your approach is calm and nonthreatening. Still, the child reacts angrily to you and refuses to do what you say; then, she immediately goes to her parent, your partner, and argues her case. If your partner feels guilty about how his child is handling the divorce, he may quickly side with her. This type of situation occurs often, and it would benefit you to recognize these behaviors if they are operating within your stepfamily.

One way to correct this kind of behavior is to see a family counselor, someone who specializes in stepfamilies. Another way is to have a family meeting and discuss how this affects your ability to function as the other adult in this home, an authority figure, and a significant member of the family. It is important that your stepchild and your partner feel safe enough to discuss this sensitive issue with you. If you come across as a caring, sensitive individual, you will achieve greater results in less time and gain the respect from your partner that you deserve.

The overprotectiveness that parents feel toward their children is a very real practice that occurs in many families of divorce or some type of separation. It is an understandable practice but also a tough thing for stepparents to work through. You need several things:

- a cooperative partner
- a genuine caring for your stepchild
- a commitment to making your stepfamily work

These emotions can also interfere with your relationship with your stepchild because your partner may feel threatened by your attempts to get close to her child. An overprotective parent is tough to work through, but this second issue is equally, if not more, difficult to get your arms around. You may be thinking, How can my partner possibly feel threatened by my wanting to get close to her child? I thought that's what being a stepfamily was all about! You're right; that is what being a stepfamily is all about. I have spoken with parents who have been embarrassed to discover that they have felt threatened by an outsider (which you are) attempting to bond with their child. It's not an insecurity on the parents' part necessarily, although this does happen in some people. Generally it appears to be more rooted in a fear that their child will reject them. The fear of rejection seems to come from the parents' feeling that their child blames them for not being together as a family anymore, and getting close to another adult may give the child permission to not rely so much on his parent. This is a confusing and difficult issue, but if you think this is what's happening in your family, let's look at some dialogue to learn how to handle your partner's insecurity.

Stepparent: I noticed tonight that when I was doing homework with Betsy alone, you weren't responding when we occasionally asked you to join us, or when we asked a question. Is my observation correct?

Parent: What do you mean? I was just reading the paper.

Stepparent: Yes, I saw that you were reading the paper, but generally you answer me when I talk to you. It felt uncomfortable when you didn't answer me.

Parent: I'm sorry that you felt uncomfortable, and you're right. I was unresponsive. I don't know how to talk to you about this.

Stepparent: I want you to be able to talk to me about anything. I'm your partner and we have this family together; how can I help you feel better about telling me this?

Parent: Well, try not to think that I'm being childish or something.

Stepparent: Alright. It's a deal.

Parent: Ever since my divorce (or whatever the situation is), I know that Betsy misses her mother a great deal. I always thought that if I found someone that Betsy could relate to and vice versa, she could depend on a family structure again. The terrific thing is that I did find someone just like that—and you have been great with Betsy, suggesting activities to do together and making time just for the two of you. The only problem is that now I feel funny about seeing you two alone, doing things together, and I'm not sure why. Sometimes I think maybe I was wrong and that Betsy should really only bond with her mother and me because that's what was familiar to her. Maybe it would be less complicated for Betsy. But that would be difficult for you. I'm really confused about this.

Stepparent: I can understand your dilemma. And I want to be included. I'm your wife, and a big part of this family. Given the way we both feel, I have a possible solution. How would you feel about asking Betsy what she thinks? If it *is* confusing for Betsy, let's ask her what we could do to encourage her relationship with her mother but also continue to build a relationship with me as her stepparent. By doing it this way, you can feel assured that you're giving Betsy what she wants, or needs, and I don't risk feeling left out.

What just happened here? Two adults in a difficult situation diplomatically compromised on a sensitive matter where emotions could easily flare at any moment. The key thing to keep in mind as a stepparent is that your partner's feelings are *paper thin* when it comes to his children, particularly if they are recently apart from their other parent. You can help mend the situation; being sensitive to your partner's feelings about his children is a major step in healing the past and rebuilding again.

Dealing with Your Partner's Emotions in a Second Marriage

Your partner is important to you, and you are important to your partner. Sometimes when people enter second marriages, they try to mask any lingering emotions that may be connected to their previous life. This is not unusual. Others may be more forthright about it—spewing anger, resentment, and guilt in the path of anyone who crosses them. What kind of partner do you have? How does he or she deal with his or her emotions? Give yourself a minute to think about this. When you met, were your first conversations about how your partner's ex-spouse did him/her wrong? How long was it before you both started discussing your past lives with other people? Or perhaps you have not had this conversation yet? Possible, but not likely. We generally love to talk about ourselves, and maybe tend to make it sound a little better or worse than it was; we try to impress someone we are attracted to and with whom we have the potential to develop a relationship.

SIGNS AND BEHAVIORS TO CLUE YOU IN

There are specific signs and behaviors, however, that can inform us when our partner feels anger, resentment, guilt, or any other emotion that could potentially threaten the future of the relationship. These signs include an avoidance of wanting to discuss the relationship, the stepfamily, or other issues clearly important to the union. Another sign is if your partner becomes easily and quickly irritated when you are discussing the future of your relationship. Or if your partner continually obsesses about his ex-spouse and the negative things that occurred, it may warrant pointing this out to him to try to correct his behavior. Beside the fact that you don't want to continue to hear this over and over, it is also not healthy for the children to hear about it repeatedly. A partner with this kind of leftover baggage must address it, accept it, and move on for the sake of success in a future relationship.

If *you* are exhibiting this kind of behavior, the same advice applies. Sometimes we don't even realize the impact of what we are saying or the repeated patterns of what and how we say things. Remember, it's always good to examine your own behaviors and patterns first before offering corrective advice to someone else, particularly a partner who lives with you!

If you feel that your partner does exhibit some of the above behaviors, how should you approach it? First of all, ask yourself this: Does this behavior bother me enough to want to do something about it? Remember the saying "Choose your battles carefully." If you feel that your partner, and you, could benefit from eliminating this behavior, a discussion is in order. Begin by choosing a flexible time and place to have this discussion. Why? It's important that your partner be receptive to having this conversation. Try not to begin the discussion at a busy time at your house or when other issues clearly distract your partner, and hide the TV remote! The conversation could go like this:

You: Honey, I'm concerned about something and I'd like to discuss it, but I need your full attention for this one. (Your partner will probably stop what he or she is doing immediately upon hearing that.)

Partner: Okay. Is it something that I've done?

You: It's something that we both need to work on. I've noticed that when we talk about your ex-spouse, there's much emotion in your voice. It sounds like anger or resentment, and I sure understand about that. The thing that concerns me, though, is that we tend to have virtually the same conversation about (ex-spouse's name) almost every time this subject comes up. Honey, I know that you feel your life before had serious problems, and I'm sorry about that. But I'm concerned about us, here and now, and the future. I feel like you're not moving on and that the issues in your past are not yet resolved. Can you see that, too?

Partner: Do I really talk about it that much? I had no idea. I guess I've gotten so used to feeling this negativity and discussing it with you. You've never said anything before about it, so I figured it was okay to vent to you. I'm glad you pointed it out; I want our future to work, too. Will you help me with this? Maybe when I bring the subject up again, you could gently remind me of this conversation.

You: Are you sure that won't offend you? I know you don't like to be reminded of things sometimes.

Partner: You're right, I don't, but this is too important to us. I'll make an effort to acknowledge how you feel, and, with your help, try to stop rehashing the past negative stuff.

Keep in mind that things may not change overnight. It takes time for people to change, so allow yourselves that time. Releasing the past is probably one of the most difficult tasks we can face, especially if that past was painful. Our past was something familiar that belonged to us. We all have difficulty parting with familiarity—please try to remember that if you feel your partner isn't letting go fast enough. And your partner may not be able to change the behavior completely. Ask yourself what you are willing to tolerate. Know this ahead of time, before you have the above conversation. Also, recognize your partner's limitations. If you know what you can live with, then accept her efforts and degree of compromise, and move on. One of the most serious problems in relationships is that we tend to bring up the past again and again—even if we have discussed issues about it and *thought it was resolved.* Learn to accept what you and your relationship can withstand, and do not continue to bring it up with sarcasm and criticism. Sarcasm and criticism are not motivating; they are hurtful and can seriously damage your relationship.

Often, when we talk about letting go of the past, we think that it means *eliminating* the past. But our past helped to make us who we are today. In a stepfamily situation, we often wish and hope that our new partner will forget this past (with his ex-spouse), and start fresh and new with us. When this fails, disappointment and havoc reign because the expectation that your new partner will erase his past is unrealistic. Yes, he was married to someone else. Yes, he had a life with someone else. And, yes, he is now living with you. But that does not mean that his other life did not exist. You are a new chapter and your job is to help your partner experience a loving relationship, and to grow with you. That's his job, too, by the way. So don't think that your partner can erase or eliminate his past. Instead, acknowledge it, accept it, and celebrate the positives from it—such as the children. You probably don't want to share the negatives from your partner's past anyway, do you? So why not share the positives because you can build on them in your own new life together?

You can do more for your partner by following this plan than you'll probably ever realize!

How Can We Create a Stepfamily Plan Together?

Be honest. Have you ever asked yourself this question? Have you ever talked about this with your partner—before you got married? Did you have any idea how this stepfamily was going to work? Did you discuss your idea with your partner? Sadly, the answer I receive to this question 85 percent of the time is no. And, frankly, this should be the second question, right after Will you marry me? Can you think of anything more important than having a plan about your family's future? I can't. You must make this a priority in your life when you are about to be a stepfamily. If you don't, the results could be disastrous for you and your stepfamily members.

Why is it so important to lay out the stepfamily plan? Compare it to working on a team project at work. This team consists of people who are experts in their area, such as marketing, sales, pricing, and production. The team leader has indicated the project's goal to the other members. However, the team leader did not discuss the means of reaching that goal. So, immediately upon hearing the goal, each of the four members of the team developed four separate mental plans for how to reach the goal. Anxious to get started, the members of the team begin working on their portion of the project. No time is taken to discuss a what-happens-if scenario.

Everyone is moving along fine until, without notice, an

unexpected glitch occurs with the project. Things are at a standstill. Each member of the team begins to problem-solve, following their own mental plan. You can imagine what happens next—complete chaos. The marketing person moves forward considering only the marketing options, the sales person proceeds based solely on the sales options, and so on. The team is no longer moving forward together; everyone is off in their own direction, doing what they think is right. The result? The project fails and the only choices are to start over or scrap the entire thing, throwing away all of the hard work and effort that went into it.

The very same disappointing conclusion can occur in a stepfamily without the proper planning and collaborating. I find that people about to become a stepfamily don't necessarily think of this new adventure as a project that requires planning, forecasting, and "what if" scenarios. We tend to think of our stepfamily as something that is going to work out, no matter what. That's probably because before we become a stepfamily, most of us are on our best behavior. It's when we move in together that our real selves emerge, and sometimes that's not so attractive. Conflict occurs in all kinds of situations and the stepfamily is not an exception. Anytime we consider a major structural project with many parts, the success is measured and determined by how well the plan is thought out, and engineered.

How to Approach Developing a Stepfamily Vision

So, for those of you who are not yet a part of your stepfamily, this will be great preventative information. For those who are in the stepfamily, and did not develop the plan beforehand, this is your chance. Take it. I would suggest, first, sitting down and actually writing out each person's version of how they think this stepfamily should look. Compile the list of cast members involved, including extended family members, such as ex-spouses and grandparents. Map this out on a piece of paper showing who is related to who and who fits in where. Sometimes there are multiple stepfamily situations involved and, if you are a visual person, it can help to see what you are working within your stepfamily.

Both you and your partner need to jot down notes about how you envision handling situations in your stepfamily. For example, list categories such as Finances or Budget, Discipline, Holidays, Visitation, Household Duties, and Family Meetings. Add other categories that may apply to your specific stepfamily situation. Below each category, discuss how you each feel about it, how you have handled this previously, and how you now plan to deal with it in the stepfamily. This exercise is a tremendous eye-opener to a stepfamily-wanna-be couple. Often, people will discover things about themselves and their partners that are tremendously helpful insights, but the opposite can also occur. Be prepared to reveal some potentially not-so-pleasant information about yourself, or to hear it about your partner. But remember the point of this exercise. You must be honest because you need to start from a solid base to build this vision.

Now that you have written down your positions in the categories that will affect your stepfamily, review each position carefully to see where you agree and disagree. This exercise can be modified down the road if your situation changes. You may encounter new experiences that will add categories to your list that may require negotiation and compromise. Before you review each position, prepare to compromise because you will not agree on everything, and some give and take will undoubtedly need to take place. With compromise you can merge the positions into one vision that you each can live with and that you will need to follow in your stepfamily. Depending on how you and your partner negotiate and compromise, this process can either be smooth or difficult. You may require a mediator; an objective person who has nothing at stake in either of your positions and can help you work through this process. Be open to ideas about how you can make this work. Exercise compromise and give where you need to give. You *both* have the opportunity to express your opinions about how the stepfamily should work, and you both have input into your future, bringing in your own expertise on issues, such as in the team-project example.

Try to be proactive with your stepfamily and know the vision up front. Once your plan is developed, be responsible in sticking to it. New situations that occur don't seem so surprising or scary if you have figured out how to handle them *before* they happen. There will be situations that are not included in your plan; you cannot anticipate every event. But envisioning the major situational categories is a great start. Once you've negotiated these, you and your partner will know how to deal with future issues as well. The benefits of having already discussed your positions up front include:

- reducing any surprise situations that may lead to anger and blame
- knowing ahead of time what to expect
- having a sneak preview of how you and your partner problem solve together
- reducing the chance of conflict between you and your spouse
- increasing the chances of stepfamily success!

The shared vision for your stepfamily is one of the most important things you and your partner can do for validation of you as the stepparent. Having input from the beginning into how your stepfamily will work solidifies your position as the copartner and coparent in the stepfamily situation. Often families begin their lives together thinking about how the family will live together but not actually discussing or writing out the plan to follow. This leads us to react to situations on impulse, without having the opportunity to think through our responses before reacting. Many times this creates a problem for the stepchildren because they may see you as unpredictable, and this leaves them uncertain about what to expect from you. They will turn to their parent for help, which puts their parent in an awkward situation now having to confront you, the spouse. Better to plan ahead, and stay with the plan.

WHY IT'S IMPORTANT TO COMPROMISE

Although it is important to share the development of the vision, there is an overriding element here that we must discuss. That element is the natural influence that the parent already has when coming into the stepfamily with the children. Every parent who enters into a stepfamily has already established some kind of parenting and family pattern with their children. This pattern has been operating since the children were born, and it is familiar and well entrenched in the children's *and* the parents' lives. Enter you, the stepparent. You are a new component in this already-existing family pattern of traditions, holiday activities, communication network with extended family members, day-to-day routines, and house rules. Not only are you the new component, but you may also bring your own routines into this stepfamily. Whose patterns and traditions do you continue to use?

Understandably, one set of family patterns cannot be chosen over the other, unless, as the stepparent, you agree with whatever your spouse brings to the household. This isn't always the case, so conflict can occur if these issues are not discussed and sorted out. When two partners come to the stepfamily with their own children, the same kind of planning and negotiation should take place when looking at routines, traditions, and all of the other family patterns.

Ideally, taking something from each of the two family patterns and merging them would work the best. For example, if your spouse has always had the children for Christmas and you have always had your children for Christmas, you now have one big Christmas. If one of you have not had your children for Christmas, you have choices. You can work out a plan, instead, to find another time close to the holidays when you can all be together. If having everyone together is not important to you, then you can continue the established practice.

Before you become a stepfamily, make an effort to discuss these details. Otherwise, you may have not only your family for Christmas but your spouse's entire family, too, with little notice on how many turkeys to prepare for a holiday dinner! It's also important to talk about this in the event that you and your spouse disagree and need to restructure holidays or situations that conflict, because the stepchildren may continue to expect things to carry on as they always have. So, if you need to make any changes, inform the children of those changes so that their expectations are correct. They also may have some valid input. Planning your *new* traditions and routines can also be a stepfamily project, keeping in mind that everyone's opinion should be considered and being careful not to offend anyone's ex-spouse or ex-family members.

In the stepfamily where only one of the adults has children, I have found that it will ultimately be the parent's family pattern and outlook that will shape the stepfamily. This may sound one-sided and slightly unfair to the stepparent. Well, it is. But it is important to understand why you need to give in on this one.

From the time their children are born, or conceived, parents generally have goals and ideals planned for their children. As the children grow, the goals and ideals become cemented in the parents' minds and behavior. Parents will make decisions in their own lives based on what they want for their children. This is sometimes difficult for a stepparent without children to understand. It may even be difficult for a stepparent with children to understand, if that stepparent raised her own children differently. In any case, the parent is coming into your new stepfamily with goals and ideals he has developed for his children over many years.

I urge you to find out what these goals and ideals are! As the stepparent, you need to know your partner's plans for his children because it could affect the way you shape your stepfamily in many ways including socially, financially, and emotionally. And if you disagree with something about your partner's plans for his children, it would be wise to know about this ahead of time. It is unlikely that a parent will change or adjust the goals he has for his children just for you. So, if you disagree with them, but you can live with it, fine. If you disagree and cannot live with it, think now about how long forever is! A Mack truck could not move the plans a parent has for his child, so don't disillusion yourself into thinking that you will be able to do it! You will inflict irreparable damage on your intimate relationship if you try, and your stepchildren will sense this. Your stepchildren will then resent you for interfering, and you will lose precious bonding ground.

As the stepparent, you must understand and accept your partner's view on the previous family pattern meshing into the new stepfamily. The children have been raised with a family pattern, and it's not fair to them if they suddenly have to change everything because a new person came into their lives. That's not to say that *some* adjustment can't be tolerated. But for the most part, the biological parent and her children have a pattern of living that has probably worked for them for some time. Much of that pattern should remain intact, especially if it has worked successfully up to this point. It would be a difficult adjustment for your partner to have to change everything; it would be complicated for the stepchildren and this would present them with an opportunity to resent you—the reason for the change.

I am not suggesting that the stepparent must adopt every aspect of the previous family pattern. If you are uncomfortable with something, talk to your partner about it. Your partner should be receptive to at least hearing your concern, and, if reasonable, be willing to make adjustments. For example, if your partner invites his ex-spouse over for dinner every Sunday and expects you to cook, and this bothers you, you should speak up.

Sharing Emotional Vision

What is emotional vision and why is it important to share? Emotional vision is the future of your stepfamily and how both you and your partner *feel* about it. In our culture, we sometimes harbor an assumption when people marry that both parties feel the same about their future. When couples figure out that it isn't really that way, the turbulence begins. We are all aware of the divorce rate. It's no different for stepfamilies. In working with stepfamilies, I've found that it's even more crucial that the members of the stepfamily have this emotional vision about themselves and their new family members, and that all members share this vision. Make an investment in your stepfamily. Make it work and stick to it. Plan beforehand to try to prevent surprises and problems down the road. One way to achieve this is to establish and share an emotional vision.

Try this exercise. Think about each member of your stepfamily. Write down their names on a piece of paper, allowing each name its own column. In the columns, jot down five adjectives to describe each member. This is solely your observation, and you can go back and redo this exercise from time to time—as your emotional vision changes. Once you've written the adjectives to describe your stepfamily member, do the same for yourself. Jot down five adjectives you know to be true about yourself. Then write five adjectives of how your stepfamily members might describe you. Under each of the former columns, write one sentence about how you feel about that stepfamily member. Now, under each column, write one sentence about how you would describe him or her to someone else. For example, start something like, "I feel my stepdaughter, Alex, is (_____)." Evaluate what you have written in each column, especially noting where conflicts may occur.

This exercise is a reality check. Our feelings can be volatile, and you need to be completely honest. Your partner should complete the same exercise. Once you are finished, compare notes.

Discuss any questions or concerns. The purpose for sharing is to reveal to each other the precise emotion that you are feeling about each member of the family. This may be new information for one or both of you. It is intended to enhance your understanding how each of you feels about your stepfamily. Once you have shared this information, you will each have an understanding of where you stand, which constitutes a starting point. You can then begin to discuss where you feel your stepfamily can go, and what your future can feel like.

I worked with a stepfamily that was experiencing problems shortly after the marriage. Abigail had never been married before she married Craig, who had three children from his previous marriage. Things were going along smoothly until a change occurred in the visitation schedule, and Craig's three kids were now in the house more often. At first, the kids were at Craig and Abigail's one weekend a month and every Wednesday. Due to a change in Craig's ex-spouse's employment, the kids were now coming every weekend and an additional day during the week. Abigail found this quite difficult to adjust to, and she and Craig began quarreling more often.

As both partners talked, Abigail revealed that she was experiencing a problem with how she felt about the kids, and their sudden increase in visitation served to exacerbate her feelings. She could handle the first visitation schedule without much difficulty, but the revised schedule caused their life to change quite a bit, and she wasn't emotionally willing to accept the children into their lives on an increased basis. Abigail tried to adjust her feelings about this and felt guilty about the way she felt, which only added to the frustration. Craig worked out the schedule with his ex-spouse and consulted Abigail very little on this big change. Abigail resented Craig for handling it this way.

As a result, we had a stepparent who was frustrated with her partner; one, for not including her in the decision about increased visitation, which had a direct affect on her life, and two, because she did not feel emotionally ready to accept three children on an increased basis into her life with her new partner. Abigail was fine when she could count on the one weekend and every Wednesday, but the change in her own life, with the increased schedule, made her feel angry and resentful of the children. Abigail had envisioned a life predominantly alone with Craig—she saw the children as an extension that came infrequently to visit. Craig, on the other hand, envisioned—and hoped—that someday his kids would be able to visit him even more, and maybe live with him full-time. When Craig mentioned that, the color drained out of Abigail's face.

At that moment, I knew that this topic had not been discussed prior to the marriage. Abigail had no idea what Craig had wanted for his children. Throughout future sessions, we did the exercise above and Abigail revealed how she really felt about members of the stepfamily. From that information, Craig and Abigail began rebuilding the structure and emotional vision of their future together. This time, their visions were clear to each other, and although it a painful experience, the marriage survived. One of the important things for Abigail to accept was that Craig wanted his kids to live with them more often. It had not occurred to her earlier that the ex-spouse's life would change and that Craig would need to take more of the parenting responsibility. Abigail felt that things would continue the way they had been, until the kids moved out on their own. It was an oversight on Abigail's part, and an excellent example of why it's important to accept your partner's view, to share emotional vision for the stepfamily, and how unexpected events can change the entire future course of your stepfamily.

3

STEP THREE

Understand Your Stepchild's View

"I'm always concerned with what my stepchildren think of me. I'm the adult and the parent, married to their mother, and I worry a lot about whether I'm saying something wrong or doing something wrong. I want to be a good stepparent, but how do I know how I'm doing?"

Unlike exams at school or performance evaluations at work, it's not easy to know your progress as a stepparent; most likely, your stepchildren will not give you a report card, and your spouse might tell you only positives, not wanting to risk hurting your feelings. Although this is a thoughtful thing to do, it is not realistic. As a stepparent, you want and need to know how you are doing. Are you successful as a stepparent or do you feel like a failure much of the time? Ultimately, your evaluation might be based on your own subjective information. However, this may not be accurate from your family's point of view.

It is essential that you understand your stepchild's view toward you as a stepparent. Disregarding your stepchildren's thoughts, points of view, and feelings in general is a mistake, and it can prove costly to your relationships with your spouse and her children. In my work, I have talked with many stepparents who were experiencing difficulty in their stepfamilies. Most of the stepparents are thoughtful and terrific people who sincerely want to make the relationship work, and, ultimately, want the stepfamily situation to work. They care about their spouse and they also care about their stepchildren. Then there are the other stepparents, who come in looking for someone to fix the family because there is conflict between the stepparent and stepchild. I probably don't have to describe the latter type to you; they clearly represent the challenge to a family therapist.

This chapter covers the benefits of connecting with your stepchild, and how you feel about your stepchild. In addition, the chapter takes a look at what stepkids often think, and how to find out what specific things *your* stepchild thinks—and how to connect with him regarding his thoughts.

The Benefits of Connecting with Your Stepchild

There are serious benefits that you will enjoy once you successfully connect with your stepchild. By expressing a desire to understand his feelings, you will add a newfound direction of trust and communication that will lead to a closer family unit.

Your efforts will encourage him to open up to you more readily, and you will begin to truly know this new child in your life.

Trust

Making the attempt to connect with your stepchild will send a message to her that you are interested. If a stepchild thinks you are even slightly interested in what she feels and thinks, she will feel a friendship beginning to build, and with that feeling comes an initial trust of you. Trust is the first link you must build with your stepchild. Trust will pave the way for future openness in your relationship.

Acceptance

A stepchild is concerned about whether his stepparent will accept him. You will need to initiate the feelings of acceptance with your stepchild. You can accomplish this by telling your stepchild that you understand and accept him as part of the "package" of your relationship with your spouse.

Reduced conflict

If you are aware of how your stepchild thinks and feels, your chances for conflict are reduced significantly, with your stepchild *and* your spouse. This is because, by knowing this, you will know what to avoid and how to precisely plan your verbal approach to issues.

Increased communication

If your stepchild *knows* that you are interested in what she thinks, she will feel more comfortable in talking with you about a variety of topics. Don't expect your stepchild to immediately share her most inner thoughts. That may take time, and you need to be patient.

Increased stepfamily cohesiveness

Being aware of each other's thoughts and feelings when interacting will help cement the bond of the stepfamily because you will be sensitive and careful to not offend one another or be unintentionally critical. You must take care in your interactions within the stepfamily, paying close attention to how you are stating things and how your behavior is received by others in the family.

The Dangers of Ignoring Your Stepchild's Opinion

There is danger in disregarding your stepchild's viewpoint. You run the risk of building a wall between you and your stepchild. You can prevent this from happening by not making decisions that affect your stepchild without considering what he has to say about it. You also risk having to guess what your stepchild is thinking.

If you choose not to engage in conversation or interaction with your stepchild, and silence takes over, you will both start to invent what the other is thinking. And as human beings, it is common that these thoughts we create about each other, without knowing each other, are generally negative. Do everything in your power to avoid this at all levels and open the path to building and maintaining a relationship with your stepchild.

Marianne felt that when her stepdaughters called and only spoke to their father, they were not interested in talking with her, too. When she asked her husband, McKenzie, about it, he said it wasn't a big deal and she shouldn't worry about it. But it happened again and again, and soon Marianne felt quite alienated from her stepdaughters *and* McKenzie because of what she felt was his "lack of concern." Marianne started thinking that her stepdaughters did not like her and these thoughts escalated into the feeling that she should leave the relationship! One night she confronted McKenzie about separating, and his reaction was one of shock. He had no idea that Marianne was feeling so strongly about this. It turned out that Marianne's stepdaughters also felt that *she* was the one who did not want to talk with them. A complete misunderstanding that needed a speedy resolution. Never underestimate the power of communication.

How Do You Feel About Your Stepchild?

Take a few minutes right now, before you read on, and examine how you feel about your stepchildren. It's customary in our society to respond immediately with, "Well, I love them, of course." Come on folks, these are stepchildren we're talking about, and it's okay if you don't "love" them. We'll address that more completely in Chapter Seven. I am asking you to be completely honest about how you feel about your stepchild. You don't have to say it out loud. You don't have to verbalize it to anyone. Just be honest with yourself (maybe for the first time), and determine, right now, a word or phrase that describes how you really feel about your stepchild. Write it down. Now that you are clear about your own feelings, ask yourself, Do the thoughts and feelings of my stepchild matter to me? I hope that you will answer yes to this question. If you answer no, or not really, it's going to be difficult to develop a bond with your stepchild. If you truly believe that the thoughts and feelings of your stepchild don't matter, in effect, you are ignoring an important factor in the success of your stepfamily, and your willingness to understand your stepchild's point of view is minimal.

Getting to Know Your Stepchild

It's important for you, as the stepparent, to focus on how your stepchild thinks and feels about things, not on changing how she thinks and feels. Stepchildren have experienced one of life's most difficult challenges—the ending of their nuclear family. You may think this is none of your business; make it your business. For example, it's important to know how your stepchildren feel about what happened to throw them into this stepfamily thing in the first place. It could have been a divorce of their parents, perhaps a death of a parent, or another event that would have prompted a long-term separation of their parents.

You can run for Stepparent of the Year, but you will not take that walk down the runway if your stepchild is angry and confused, possibly about something that you know nothing about! She could be angry about something that happened long before you came on the scene. Not resolved, this anger or confusion or whatever emotion she's carrying can turn into resentment— probably toward you as the newcomer or the outsider. Face it—you're an easy target because you are not genetically connected to her. It's easy to blame people who are strangers. To deal with this resentment through understanding, get to know your stepchild. Remain open to whatever your stepchild thinks or feels. Do not judge. Work on your relationship with her because more contact leads to a better understanding of one another.

You can get to know your stepchild in the following ways:

- Share a meal together
- Share time alone, just talking about your stepchild's day at school
- Offer to drive him to school one day to spend some time together
- Try to help her with her homework (if she wants you to)

Engaging in everyday activities with your stepchild will allow him to get to know you. A trust will develop so that he can feel comfortable and safe in confiding in you or in just realizing that you are not the person that may have broken up his old life, the one with *both* parents in it. You are now an addition to his life.

One caution—resist the urge to bond too soon or too quickly with your stepchild. It takes time to build trust. Be patient and allow that to occur naturally.

HOW TO START A DISCUSSION WITH YOUR STEPCHILD

If you haven't done so, make it a point to have a discussion with your stepchild, particularly about the event that catapulted her into being a stepchild. You might be surprised at what you find out (not only about her but about how she feels about you). And, in the process, you will be setting the stage for strengthening your relationship or, perhaps, beginning a relationship with your stepchild. Even if she doesn't vocalize her appreciation for asking her how she feels about this, you will develop an understanding of her thought processes about major events in her life, and you'll begin to understand what happened in her world when her parents divorced—and ultimately why she behaves as she does.

Now, it's possible that you have a stepchild who is wary of expressing her feelings to anyone—not just you. That's okay. Be patient. It may take two or three times or more to initiate conversation with your stepchild. Once she feels comfortable with trusting what you are going to do with the information (such as not tell her parent, your spouse), she will probably open up to you. However, if she wants to tell you something that may be harmful to her, you may want to set the ground rules about what you need to share with her parent.

There are several different approaches to starting a conversation with your stepchild. Generally it is good to start a conversation when the two of you are alone together. This allows both of you to be focused and not distracted by other people, particularly your spouse, whom the stepchild may defer to during the conversation. You should initiate the conversation with a simple How are you? or How is your day going?, and follow up with questions about an activity that she is currently involved in at school or at work. As much as possible, let your stepchild do the talking. Kids like to talk about themselves, so if you allow this, you will find out much information about your stepchild.

Carrie's stepdaughters had brief and painfully nice encounters with her for the first one or two years of their life together. To Carrie, it seemed like forever until her stepdaughters were comfortable talking and asking her about her life, without Carrie always feeling the need to initiate conversations. The reason for this was very real to her stepdaughters—they were comparing her to their experiences with their other stepparent. Once Carrie's stepdaughters realized that her approach was different and more stepdaughter-friendly, they opened up and conversation flowed more smoothly. This was something Carrie did not instinctively know but learned in observation over time. She does not consider herself a patient person and added that her partner could vouch for that, but she knew that patience was paramount to building a bond with her stepchildren and with their father, a bond-building exercise well worth the wait.

Conversation Starters That Get Stepkids Talking Include

- How is your mom (or dad)? Asking about their other parent may seem sticky, but my experience in doing this has been surprisingly positive. For example, stepparents have reported that when the stepchildren return from a visit with their other parent, they often want to talk about it. Asking them about their mom or dad lights them up, and they feel at ease. Why? Because their stepparent is asking them about their own parent—somebody they thought their stepparent couldn't care less about and is not supposed to like! Showing interest in their other parent allows the stepchildren to feel comfortable with you—they don't have to walk on eggshells because they just returned from "the other place."

- Compliment and inquire about their clothing or their looks. For a male, say something such as "I like that jacket. Where did you get it?" For a female child, comment on her appearance. "What an interesting color of nail polish. What color is that?"
- What school activities are you involved in?
- Humor helps. Try to incorporate it into your questions.
- Develop a rapport by trying to keep the conversation superficial and not getting too heavy right away. Ask a question like, "This feels weird, you and I talking alone, huh? Do you feel as uncomfortable as I do?"
- Go slow. If you go too fast you will lose them. Ask one question at a time.

YOU MAY NEED YOUR PARTNER'S HELP

If all else fails to engage a conversation with your stepchild, consider gleaning information about her feelings from your spouse. Ask your partner to give you his impression of how his child thinks and feels. This is an invaluable exercise, not only to understand your stepchild but also your partner's feelings about his child. You will now have an understanding of your partner's decisions when they seem confusing to you. However, one drawback is that sometimes the parents have conflicting views as well, and the goal is to obtain accurate information so that you draw your own conclusions.

I would caution that if you choose this method, you should be cognizant of the fact that your partner may be giving you his impression of how the child feels, which may not be completely accurate. I suggest discussing this with your partner only as a starting point for you. The ideal step then would be to initiate a three-way conversation with you, your partner, and your stepchild, after gathering as much information as you can. This may seem time-consuming to you, but think of it as an investment in your stepfamily's future. Stepchildren tend to want to discuss issues as a family, so take advantage of one-on-one discussions and discussions as a stepfamily whenever you can.

LuAnn and Allen had been married for about six months when it became painfully clear to LuAnn that Allen's children did not seem comfortable engaging in a discussion or in any activities with her. She felt she had tried everything she could to get her stepson and stepdaughter to respond. Her stepson, Dayton, seemed most uncomfortable with her and, at the time, he was about to turn thirteen. The couple came in for therapy feeling exhausted and frustrated with the situation. After much discussion with LuAnn, Allen, and the children, it became clear that LuAnn's stepson felt he was betraying his mother, even when he only participated in a conversation with his stepmother. LuAnn and Allen were given specific "homework" assignments to work together in helping Dayton understand that his mother will always be his mother, and LuAnn is a significant part of the stepfamily and only wants to be an *additional* support to him. Once Dayton understood this, it removed an obstacle from the stepfamily's developing relationship, and Allen continued to support LuAnn and his son in encouraging a relationship between them. Having his father's blessing in this, Dayton responded positively to LuAnn, feeling secure that he was not betraying his mom.

Common Thoughts And Feelings Stepchildren Have

Although each stepchild is unique as an individual, there are thoughts and feelings that stepchildren have in common, sharing the same experience of being raised in a stepfamily. Whether it's imagining that their parents will reunite or feeling overprotective of their parents, knowing these thoughts ahead of time can reduce your own anxiety when you encounter them. Sometimes stepchildren need to work through some of their feelings before moving on and accepting you into their family.

THEIR PARENTS WILL GET BACK TOGETHER

Stepchildren fantasize about their parents someday getting back together. Actually, although I refer to it as a fantasy, it may seem quite real to stepchildren. However, it's not realistic, especially when you are married to one of the parents of these children who are fantasizing! (Or at least I hope it's not realistic, for the survival of your relationship.) It's not unhealthy for children to dream about their parents getting back together. Adults whose parents divorced when they were children find themselves wondering what it would be like if their parents were back together again. So, it's not uncommon for children (or adult children) to wish their parents would reunite. Depending on the age of the stepchildren, however, some of these feelings are due to their inability to understand adult relationships. For adult children, it is often a need to have things return to the way they were, in a comfortable place with both parents intact as a home base.

In the early part of Andrea's relationship with Tim, she was not as familiar with a parent's connection to his ex-spouse when raising the children separately. Andrea found herself thinking that Tim and his ex-spouse seemed to be in touch with each other so often that a reunion might be a possibility. Andrea knows now that their frequent contact was for the children, but at times it seemed excessive. Andrea felt more insecure in the beginning of the relationship. She later realized that it is important to examine all the factors when trying to understand why you feel certain emotions.

Bothered by these events, and after talking with Tim about how to resolve this, Andrea decided one day to ask her stepdaughters (with Tim's permission) if they had visions of their parents getting back together. Their answer reassured her. One abruptly said, "No!" The other one just said, "No, I don't think so," and gave Andrea that look of, Are you crazy? So, although the stepdaughters might have thought it was a strange question, it was worth asking and helped Andrea to realize that she was seeing the situation in the wrong way. Andrea shared this information with Tim, and he too, was surprised at his children's responses. Interestingly, Andrea recently shared with me that Tim told her that for a long time after the divorce, his children did wish he and their mother would get back together. He just assumed that they still felt that way. Prior to Andrea's arrival in the family, however, the stepchildren had come to the realization that their parents would remain apart.

Have this discussion with your stepchildren if they have made a comment or if something triggered this thought for you. It's a good idea to clear this with your partner first, however, in the event that it's a sensitive subject. Remember, it's easier to ask for clarity than to assume you know the facts. This is too important in building a bond with your stepchildren. They will be leery of you anyway; why not help them help you clarify things? It's likely they will be surprised at the question, and they may think you are quite perceptive in addressing something they were thinking but had no intention of voicing.

If your stepchildren indicate a desire for their parents' reunion, you may feel disappointed. That's understandable. Try not to take it personally. Their desires for their parents' reunion probably don't have anything to do with you as a person; the idea of their parents together is familiar to them, and many of us feel comfortable with familiarity.

THE STEPPARENT IS AN OUTSIDER

Stepchildren are cautious about investing time in their parent's new partner because they view the stepparent as a temporary outsider to the family system. They often see the stepparent as someone who interferes with established routines and relationships. One of the most difficult things to understand about a stepfamily is that children give unconditional love and trust to their parent, but feel that the stepparent must earn their love and trust over time. This is not often communicated and can be especially painful for stepparents who are childless themselves. Remember, parents don't *have* to compromise—they have their child's unconditional love. Stepparents do have to compromise—your love and respect must be earned.

THE NEED TO PROTECT THEIR PARENT

Another common feeling that stepchildren have is the need to protect and defend their biological parent whenever a conflict arises—especially a conflict between the two adults. Stepchildren are often overprotective of their parents. If they hear you arguing with their parent, they may step in and defend their parent. In this instance, the stepchildren take on an adult role thinking they are *helping* their parent when, in fact, this may only serve to frustrate you. If this occurs, the parent must explain to her child that the discussion is between the spouse and stepparent and the child needs to remove himself from it.

UNLIMITED ACCESS TO THEIR PARENT

Stepchildren feel that they should have access to their parent at any time. Although all children feel this to some extent, it appears to be more prevalent with stepchildren because they need to adjust to role changes. Stepchildren, however, want their role to be the same in the stepfamily as it was in the biological family. After their recent emotional unheaval, they want access to their parent at any time because they crave stability and reassurance.

In one particular case, Holly complained about the lack of privacy in the bedroom. The stepchild, Ellen, had the uncanny timing of interrupting right at the crucial moment of intimate activity. Not accustomed to this, Holly found this frustrating, and frankly, intolerable. Her husband was not sure how to deal with this issue with the child. Prior to Holly's marriage to Frasier, his children could enter the bedroom without notice. Holly was frustrated to the point of considering leaving the relationship. Frasier resolved the situation by working through it with Ellen. Frasier explained the importance of his relationship with Holly and how this constant interruption was upsetting to him because Holly wanted to leave the relationship.

In this case, Ellen was not aware of what this was doing to her parent, and once she knew, she modified her behavior without hesitation. More specifically. the child needed to respect the adults' time in the bedroom. The family established that after a specific time each evening, in this case 9:30 P.M., the stepchild would respect the privacy of the adults and not walk into the bedroom. They also decided that the bedroom was off limits at any time unless the stepchild announced her arrival by knocking. The same method applied to the adults, specifically the stepparent entering the stepchild's bedroom. One advantage for the stepparent in this case was that the stepchild was required to clean her own bedroom!

Dealing with Stepkids' Anger, Resentment, Fear, and Confusion

Stepchildren sometimes experience negative feelings about their parents' partners based on previous experiences with mom's or dad's "friends." These negative feelings can be the result of feeling anger, resentment, confusion, and fear about what to expect next. Much of this negativity is the result of one emotion—fear—which can be the root cause for any anger, resentment, and confusion your stepchild may be experiencing. Why do stepchildren have this fear in relation to their stepparents? The most obvious reason might be that the stepchild has had a bad experience with someone his parent dated previously. Maybe that person's approach put fear into the stepchild because of how he or she reacted to something the stepchild said or did. The stepchild might just be shy and fears any response from an adult. Whatever the cause for this fear, separating negative feelings about you from responses to things that took place before you entered the scene is important for a stepparent's sanity.

Stepchildren may not differentiate you from other people their parent has dated in the past. The problem with this perception is that stepchildren then see all people that their parents date as the same person, and if they did not have a good impression of a previous date, then they may lump all dates together in that don't-like category. That includes you. If your stepchild talks in a negative manner about the previous people your spouse has dated, you may just let this pass, thinking that it doesn't apply to you. Unfortunately, sometimes a stepchild, in expressing negativity about someone from the past, may also be including you. For example, if your stepchildren suddenly blurt out that dad's former girlfriend wasn't a good housekeeper, this may be their way of getting a message to you. This is an example of only one incident that may signal that your stepchildren may be experiencing anger, resentment, fear, and confusion.

There are various signs and behaviors that you can watch for that may indicate that your stepchild is reacting to events that took place long ago. This can cause confusion for both you and the stepchild. A key sign is when your stepchild compares you to former people your spouse has dated, usually in a negative way as mentioned above. Another sign is that your stepchild is intentionally pointing out observations about previous people your spouse has been with, simply to irritate you. Sometimes a stepchild may feel that if he brings up the others often enough, the current stepparent will get annoyed, tire of it, and leave. The stepchild may be reacting to past relationships that weren't pleasant for him and/or to his desire to have his parent all to himself. But how do you separate your stepchild's negative feelings from the past and you? Two key ways are through example by behavior and through having a dialogue about it.

EXAMPLE BY BEHAVIOR

Example by behavior simply means being yourself. The more time you spend with your stepchild, the more opportunities your stepchild has to see you as the person you are and not as that other person her parent dated. You may, of course, have traits similar to others, but what are the chances of you being exactly like the last person your spouse dated? Also, while spending time with your stepchild, say or do things that will cement you into her mind and set you apart from anyone else. This may be something as simple as having direct eye contact with your stepchild when you talk with her—she'll remember you doing this because it will make her feel that you are interested in what she has to say. You could also take her to a place that she'll never forget. For example, I knew a stepparent who took her oldest stepdaughter to her first rock concert. The stepchild was safe with the stepparent there, it was a rock group the stepchild *loved*, and the stepchild has not forgotten that rock concert to this day (it was over eight years ago!). Or, it could be anything in between those two ideas. The key is that your stepchild sees you as an individual and not a body with just another face.

HAVING A DIALOGUE

Another way to separate your stepchild's past memories from you is to have a dialogue about it. This discussion could potentially be sensitive, so you need to be aware of that. The conversation could go something like this:

Stepparent: I notice that you talk a lot about Judith, your dad's last girlfriend.

Stepchild: Yeah, so?

Stepparent: Well, I don't think you liked her very much.

Stepchild: She was okay. What makes you say that?

Stepparent: Well, so far, I've heard about her crooked teeth,
                that she gained a few pounds while she was dating
                your dad, and that her car was a "wreck." It makes
                me wonder if you tell your friends stuff like that
                about me. I sure hope not. I love your father and
                I like spending time with you. (Your stepchild is
                now able to see that you are a human being, with
                feelings, and that you can be hurt.)

Stepchild: Just because I said stuff about Judith doesn't mean
                that I say that about you, too. Besides Dad didn't
                like Judith much and I know he really loves you.
                (Your stepchild will want to try to please you here.)

Stepparent: That's really nice of you to say how you think your
                Dad feels about me. It makes me feel better.

This is a way of opening up the conversation to give your stepchild the message that:

- He/she shouldn't be talking about Judith or anybody else
  negatively
- You have noticed this about his/her conversation
- You have feelings, and maybe, just maybe, you are not
  like Judith (meaning that you are a nice person who loves
  his/her parent)

In this type of dialogue, where you reveal feelings about your-self and avoid any direct accusations or blame, you make it safe for your stepchild to think through what you are saying and for him to respond without fear. This is an effective way to converse with stepchildren given the level of fear operating with the arrival of a new stepparent. Mabel, a very new stepparent of three months, wanted desperately for her stepdaughter, Lucy, to bond with her. Mabel wanted advice about how to do this, since Lucy had a history of fear when talking with new partners her father would date. Lucy would express her fear by simply shutting down and not talking at all.

We talked a lot about Lucy, the experiences she has had with other partners or stepparents, if any, and how she was respond-ing and behaving with Mabel. At one point it became necessary to include Lucy's father, Henry, in the sessions. In talking through these issues, Mabel discovered that Lucy had been hurt quite deeply by one of her father's former partners, in particular. This woman criticized Lucy often, and Lucy has had a pattern of withdrawing from conversation with adults, in general, ever since. Henry felt guilty for allowing his former partner to speak to Lucy in that way; he tried to prevent it, but he felt helpless in controlling it. Finally, when the relationship ended, Henry thought that Lucy would feel better and resume her ability to converse with others. When this did not occur, Henry felt lost and didn't know what to do about it.

When Henry and Mabel first began dating, Mabel tried talk-ing with Lucy; Lucy responded in one-answer responses and Mabel interpreted her behavior as shyness. But once married to

Henry, Mabel felt she and Lucy could have a closer relationship, and she was determined to make this happen. In her attempts to talk with Lucy, she noticed that Lucy did not talk long and always seemed to be in a hurry to go to her room or leave right away. Lucy had always been an assertive child, according to her father, so we decided to try a somewhat direct approach with Lucy. The next time Mabel tried to engage Lucy in a discussion, Mabel brought up the subject of this former partner of Lucy's father's. Lucy reacted with surprise, not knowing that Mabel even knew about that. The more Mabel expressed sympathy for Lucy because this woman had been critical and hurtful, the more Lucy softened. It took three or four more discussions for Lucy to trust Mabel's interest but Lucy gradually asked more questions and probed about Mabel's intentions. This was Mabel's first opportunity to explain to Lucy that she wanted only to get to know Lucy better, and to improve their relationship as stepmother and stepdaughter.

Throughout their discussions, it was imperative that Mabel listen to Lucy without judging her or creating a fearful environment. Mabel needed to be understanding by not mentioning specifics about the former partner or openly expressing negativity about this person. The focus was to bring Lucy back from feeling that Mabel, too, would criticize Lucy for what she was expressing. The exercise helped Mabel monitor what she was asking and how she, too, was responding to Lucy. *And*, it helped her to learn what approach worked best in relating to her stepchild and beginning to build that bond. How you communicate is central to developing a relationship with your stepchild.

Stepparents and stepchildren may see different degrees of success in their relationship, and this may be quite confusing. For example, if you feel that communication is an important factor in the relationship, and your stepchild believes that being allowed to watch television anytime she wants is a sign of success in your relationship, you can use this situation to clear up any confusion.

Stepparent: Why do you think watching television anytime is important?

Stepchild: Because I like to watch television.

Stepparent: I like to watch television, too, but I think talking one on one is really important.

Stepchild: What's so important about that?

Stepparent: Well, it gives me a chance to get to know you and for you to get to know me.

Stepchild: Why should I get to know you? You're marrying my Dad, not me.

Stepparent: But when I marry your Dad, I'm also marrying into the family and that includes you. And I'm interested in what you think and feel because I care about you, and I want to help the stepfamily work.

This is a terrific opportunity for you to explain how important communication is to you, and why. There is a slight chance that your stepchild will not be impressed by your discussion about communication. If that occurs, be sure to address the television issue (or whatever issue the stepchild introduces), take the opportunity to negotiate on the issue, and compromise if you can.

Stepchild: I want the stepfamily to work, too. So what about that television thing? Dad says I can watch television when my homework is done but sometimes he lets me watch a favorite program if I haven't quite finished. But what if Dad isn't home sometime when I want to watch a program and I have just a little homework left?

Stepparent: I agree with your Dad, and if you have most of your homework done, then you can watch your favorite program.

By using *her* example to demonstrate communication, you may have a win-win situation; you were able to open the door to communication, and she received an answer to something she had been wondering about ever since you moved in—how often can I watch television now with this stepparent living here?

Do You Know How Your Stepchild Feels About You?

Sometimes we don't ask people how they feel about us because we simply don't want to know, aren't sure of what people are going to say, or we don't care—more room for uncertainty and misinformation. It's important that your stepchild knows you as a person and not just as Mom's or Dad's partner. If the stepchild does not know you as a separate individual, it will be difficult for him to accept you as part of the family. He may see you only as an extension of his Mom or Dad. That may be okay with you, but eventually it may become a problem. As a stepparent, you may not always agree with your partner on issues that affect the family. If the stepchild thinks that you will always agree with his parent, and then an incident occurs where you suddenly don't agree, the stepchild will find this confusing. It may also become an opportunity for him to resent you, particularly if you disagree with something he wants and everyone else has agreed to—except you. You must understand how your stepchild thinks, and he must understand how you think.

The best times and situations for talking to your stepchild are when she is ready. For example, right after something exciting at school happened to her. She comes rushing home energetic and happy. That's your cue to give positive feedback and encouragement, and gradually start exploring her feelings with her. Start with her feelings about what happened at school and why she feels so excited. Conversely, if something disappointing happened that day and she is quiet and subdued, this can be a clue that she does want to talk first but is waiting for you to ask her how she feels. Once you make the first move, let her do the talking.

How to Ask about Issues, and How to Listen Carefully and Nonjudgmentally

Everyone in the stepfamily has a right to express their opinion, including the stepparent and the stepchild. Each also has a right to be understood. Learning how to express your anger or joy, or something in between, to the people that you live with is crucial. I find in stepfamilies that the cliché "agree to disagree" is probably more realistic than in any other relationship. Identifying situations that may cause conflict, working through these situations as a family, and developing a method for how to handle disagreements are critical because you do need to walk away and continue to tolerate one another; remember, you still live under the same roof, either part-time or full-time.

I have been introduced to different methods by families who have worked through conflict, such as talking openly as a family or writing a letter to the family member with whom you feel most in conflict. You can also keep a journal and compare war stories at the end of each week. Sometimes it helps to have a separation period after the frustration and anger has subsided, and the family members in conflict can then schedule time when they will discuss the issue, express their emotions, and remain in the room until all parties agree on a resolution. Think of methods that you utilize in your stepfamily to resolve conflict. Has it worked for you and your family? Are you satisfied with the results? If not, take a solution-oriented approach to the problem. What would be a win-win situation here? Better yet, ask yourself, What can I compromise to make this work? I would also encourage the stepchild and mom or dad to ask themselves this same question.

Also, when you do disagree with your partner, it is paramount that the stepchild see that her parent won't always win, that her parent's partner (you) will win sometimes, too. Nobody wins all of the time, but everybody should get to win some of the time, even in stepfamilies. Your stepchild will have an advantage in the outside world in subsequent relationships at work or in her personal life because she has already learned to discuss and share feelings, compromise, and consider others' feelings. Being a stepchild isn't all bad; maturing faster can be a benefit to her later on.

Stepchildren, prior to adulthood themselves, see a stepparent as just that—a stepparent. To them you have no life other than with their parent. You are a stepparent. Being childless, it was important for Margaret to maintain her individuality as a person, aside from the relationship with her husband, Andrew, and aside from her relationship with her stepchild. But it was clear that Margaret's stepson did not know her as a person for some time into the relationship. Margaret indicated that her stepson saw her only as "dad's wife," which was realistic given that his father had prior relationships. Not knowing how long Margaret would be in the picture, her stepson was not sure how much time to invest in getting to know her. Margaret was more anxious than her stepson because, of course, her intentions were for a longterm relationship with Andrew; something her stepson was not aware of at first. It was important to Margaret that her stepson know that she had diversified interests, different from his father's, and that he see her as an individual who could have interests similar to his own.

This is an opportunity for the stepchild to see you as independent of either of her parents. If you have a similar interest, try to develop an independent relationship with your stepchild—separate from her parent.

DO YOUR STEPCHILDREN THINK YOU ARE RIGHT FOR THEIR PARENT?

This sounds strange, I know, but there really is a point here. As we mentioned earlier, stepchildren are often protective of their parents—even from their parents' partners. Stepchildren sometimes feel the fear all over again if they hear their parent and stepparent arguing. This fear is that their parent will be hurt or the family shuffle will start again. *There might be a new partner, and the new one could be worse than this one*—hysteria can set in easily, especially if the fighting is intense, with angry voices. If the stepchild doesn't know you very well, he may get the impression from your arguments with his parent that you are a bad person and probably not a good partner choice for his parent. If he starts thinking this, you have lost round one. The difficulty here is that the stepchild is likely to always agree with his parent, whether his parent is right or wrong. There's not much we, as stepparents, can do about this, other than to accept the pre-existing relationship between the child and parent and be secure in our relationship with our partner. However, one way to minimize having your stepchild feel that you are the reason his parent is no longer married to his other parent is to explain your viewpoint to help him understand you.

Marissa was stunned the first time her stepfamily was having a discussion about something and her stepchild, Marla, agreed with Marissa's position and not her Dad's! It's not about competing and taking sides, but Marissa had grown accustomed to having her stepdaughter always agree with her parent. And when she said she understood how Marissa felt, Marissa had the strangest feeling. She suddenly recognized that stepchildren, too, are individuals and can clearly think for themselves. This was a major turning point in Marissa's relationship with her stepchild and a new opportunity to engage in discussions in which her stepdaughter had an opinion and could substantiate and support that opinion. Listen to your stepchild. It will benefit you.

Now that you have a better understanding of your stepchild's view of things, it's time to decide what kind of stepparent you want to be to your stepchild.

4

STEP FOUR

Decide What Kind of Stepparent You Want to Be

"When I married my husband, I was a childless woman, and he had three children. I was excited but nervous at the prospect of being a stepparent. I wasn't sure what to do or how the children would react to me. I wasn't even sure where to go for help."

This is one of the most common concerns with a new stepparent. Think back to when you first knew that you were going to be a stepparent. Remember how you felt? It was probably new and exciting. But was it also somewhat confusing? You ask yourself where the stepparent handbook is, and you find out that there isn't one! So, if there is no instruction manual, we need to create our own custom handbook, relating specifically to our own stepfamilies. This chapter will help you explore what kind of stepparent you want to be, and, as a result, you will create your very own stepparent handbook.

What Is a Stepparent?

Stepparents do not fit one mold; there are different types of stepparents just as there are different types of parents. You may need to identify, for yourself, what kind of stepparent you want to be and work toward achieving the characteristics of that vision.

First, it might help to examine what being a stepparent means to you. Take a minute and write down three responsibilities that you have as a stepparent. Once you've completed this list, prioritize the three responsibilities. This will give you an idea of what is most important to you in your role as stepparent and how these responsibilities fit into the various stepparenting styles.

As you examine the stepparenting styles in this chapter, you may find that you fit into one in particular, or you may not fit into any of them. Be creative. If you don't find a style here that you feel comfortable with, feel free to develop one of your own. A style customized to your specific stepfamily will enhance your bonding experience.

Stepparenting Styles

Most stepparents are diligent about being a good stepparent. In my work with stepparents, I have observed several styles of stepparenting that seem to operate in stepfamilies today. These styles include the superwoman/superman stepparent identity, the detached stepparent, the really-want-to-be-there-for-you-but-don't-know-how stepparent, the stepparent who wants only to participate with his stepchild as a friend and not an authority figure, and the stepparent who wants to parent just like the birth parent. All of these stepparenting styles have positive characteristics. After you have reviewed these styles, you may adapt one of them, take what you need from one or more, or find characteristics in them to build a style of your own. Or your own style may be completely separate from these five styles, built on characteristics that work best for you in your stepfamily. These styles serve as a roadmap for you to follow as you design your own model.

SUPERMAN/SUPERWOMAN STEPPARENT

The superman/superwoman stepparent is just that—he/she wants to be all things to all people in the stepfamily, particularly the stepchild. This is an honorable idea, but an incredibly busy one. The super stepparent does not want to be accused of being the wicked stepparent. There certainly is a degree of comfort in that. This type of stepparent wants to avoid conflict, and often tries to smooth things over. She wants to maintain harmony, and if you can do that as a stepparent, congratulations, because it can be extremely difficult in traditional families. And with the added stressors in stepfamilies, maintaining harmony could very well be the eighth wonder of the world!

But there are some potential downsides to being a super stepparent. This stepparent may be so preoccupied with having things go smoothly in the stepfamily that she neglects her own needs. For example, some days things may not go according to schedule, and you may want to scream. That could be a healthier alternative for helping yourself than being entirely focused on keeping peace in the family. You need to determine how far you can go with stepparenting. If you model yourself after this type, I would encourage you to listen to your own needs as well.

We can be better stepparents if our own needs are met. Another possible downside to this stepparenting type is that you may be trying to fix everything, including things that you cannot control. This is not only frustrating but also lacks satisfaction. Choose what you can work with and fix, and what you cannot. Don't try to tamper with pre-existing habits or pre-established routines. You must examine the impact of your actions, and make a decision about what can work in your own stepfamily.

THE DETACHED STEPPARENT

Another style of stepparenting is the stepparent who separates himself from the stepchild and what is happening in the stepfamily. This style is called the detached stepparent. In this style, you choose to be minimally involved with your stepchild's life. This style is not often the initial way a stepparent chooses to be a stepparent; it is usually the result of feeling like you've failed as a stepparent and have not successfully bonded with your stepchild. Generally, with this style there is little to no positive interaction between the stepparent and the stepchild. As a result, animosity and alienation most often occur between the stepparent and the stepchild.

This style certainly can hinder your opportunities to bond with your stepchild. But you may also gain by choosing this style. How? Well, you could probably avoid a lot of time spent thinking about your stepchild and how you could positively influence her development. Or you could save yourself the feelings of worry or perhaps guilt over disciplinary situations that occur between you and your stepchild. However, I urge you to evaluate the entire situation thoroughly first. Think of what you will lose if you choose this style—the opportunity to parent a terrific stepchild, the opportunity for a stepchild to look up to you, and the opportunity to deepen the relationship between you and your spouse, whose child is a big part of his life.

THE UNCERTAIN STEPPARENT

This style is usually adopted by stepparents who have not had previous experience in parenting prior to becoming a stepparent. An uncertain stepparent may not know whether to discipline or not to discipline; feeling guilty if she does discipline and feeling as though her stepchild will feel she doesn't care about him if she fails to discipline or acknowledge his behavior. This is an uncomfortable position primarily because indecision is confusing, and it promotes inconsistency with your actions as a stepparent. For example, if you discipline your stepchild on one particular occasion and not on another under the same circumstances, it will confuse your stepchild—and you. Your stepchild may begin to not take you seriously, and that can deeply affect your ability to stepparent.

The positives of this style are that you care enough about your stepchild's feelings to be concerned about the effects of discipline; the drawback is that stepchildren need consistency in an adult role model. If you are leaning toward this style of stepparenting, you need to consider the impact of your potentially confusing responses to your stepchild and to your partner. And remember, there is complexity in the stepfamily anyway; this style could add to that chaos and complicate things further for all members of the stepfamily.

THE FRIEND STEPPARENT

The friendship style is often chosen as the last resort by stepparents, primarily because they simply do not know how to be anything else to their stepchildren. This happens when your partner is not supportive or able to lend assistance and guidance to you in your role. This also occurs if, as a stepparent, you don't feel comfortable in taking on the parenting role, or if you simply do not want to interfere with your partner and his ex-spouse's parenting styles.

Many stepparents are also fearful of appearing to be the "wicked" stepparent; often avoidance seems to resolve that. There is one healthy and positive feature of this stepparenting style. Being a friend to your stepchild does appear to allow stepparents to accept their stepchildren more readily. Being friends may result in feeling as if you are equals. However, this is not the case in all stepparent-stepchild relationships. You must examine your situation to determine the success potential of this or any of the other styles mentioned. Being a friend to your stepchildren does eliminate some of the complications. A problem may occur, however, with your partner over this one. For example, even though you and your stepchild are friends, there will be times when your stepchild will have an opinion on something, and as your friend, will want your support. If your spouse disagrees and also wants your opinion, you may need to be prepared to mediate, balance, or diplomatically excuse yourself from that position. Ultimately you are married to your spouse, your stepchild's parent, and he is the person who will want you on his side, for better or for worse. It is a balancing phenomenon, and as the stepparent, you may find yourself in situations where you need to be the master negotiator.

STEPPARENT AS PARENT

If your goal as a stepparent is to be a parent to your stepchild, be sure that you are up to the challenge. This may require more patience over a longer period of time. You are likely to experience much trial and error with this because your authority as parent may not be taken seriously, at least initially, by your stepchild. You will need to experiment with what works and what doesn't. Your experiments, however, may be at the expense of your stepchild, so you must be prepared before you become a "parent"!

The key to your success will ultimately be the support of your spouse. Why? Because your spouse will need to give you his permission to be a parent to his child. Being a parent to your stepchild means that you will have a direct effect on her life, not only in her development now, but also in how she will conduct herself in the future. As her parent, you will have contributed to her character and personality and how she views herself, other people, and the world. Think of the weight of that gift. If your spouse trusts you enough to be a parent to his child, you should take this responsibility seriously. This will require a good deal of thought and planning. There will be big decisions and small decisions; there will be joy and there will be disappointment. Being a parent is the toughest and most rewarding stepparent style and you must be certain that you can handle this role. Do not decide to implement this style on a whim—be prepared to follow through or you will only confuse your stepchild.

In addition to the styles mentioned above, there are myths that are floating around out there about stepparents, particularly among stepchildren. One of these longstanding myths is that all stepparents are evil. We know that is not entirely true, but it is our responsibility to convince our stepchildren of this! Another common myth is that stepparents do not listen to their stepchildren, do not care about their stepchildren, and do not like their stepchildren's other parent. The ultimate myth is that stepparents are not human. I love that one, and it's generally a little easier to dispel than the others!

At one time or another, as stepparents, we have probably all encountered one or more of these myths. Take the time now to think of additional situations in your stepfamily where stepparenting myths have been allowed to exist. How have you handled them? This is a tough situation for any stepparent. Much of the myth in our role can be eliminated through our behaviors and actions. Stepchildren are observant and watchful of their stepparents. As I've discussed in earlier chapters, you need to be cognizant of your actions around your stepchildren. Also, monitor your verbal responses to situations in your stepfamily. Above all, be yourself because that will demonstrate, to your stepchildren, the human being that you are. I would encourage you to enlist your partner's help in dispelling some of these stepparenting myths to your stepchildren. Your stepchild will be more likely to see you as your spouse sees you—particularly, if your spouse re-enforces "who you are" to her child.

How Do You Fit into Your Stepfamily?

Do you feel sometimes that you simply don't fit into this situation? Guess what, you are not alone. Most stepparents feel this way at times. How can you feel that you don't fit into your own family? This is one of those differences between traditional families and stepfamilies. A stepfamily is a family, yes, but it is a family put together like a puzzle—it's not homegrown like the traditional family. In a stepfamily, the pieces must fit together for the family to feel comfortable together. But if, as a stepparent, you feel that you don't fit, your family's chances for unity are diminished. Many stepparents feel left out. The other members of your family have a previous history and their routines need to be modified to include another person. Sometimes you may feel awkward because you are the reason for all the adjustment and change.

Stepparents can feel like outsiders for a variety of reasons. Your partner may have a conversation with his child, and you may feel excluded, or your stepchild may want to participate in an activity with *just her parent*, and you may feel left out. Former relatives may visit and you can't relate to anything they say because it all happened before your arrival! Whatever the reason, it is natural for a stepparent to feel excluded at times. So, how do you deal with feeling left out in your own family?

First, you need to ensure that you *feel* you are an integral part of this stepfamily. You, as the stepparent, already are an important asset to the stepfamily. But do you feel that you are an asset to this stepfamily? Often, stepparents overlook the significance of their role in the stepfamily. You are many things to many people. To your spouse you are an intimate partner, soulmate, and companion. To the stepchildren you are an additional adult role model, someone to help them through the rough spots of growing up—someone who has already been there. Yes, their parents provide that role, too, perhaps, but you are an objective adult role model. Stepchildren tend to look up to their stepparent, once they know and trust you. So, by understanding the role that you play, you can begin to comprehend how you fit into your stepfamily and stop feeling left out.

You can also eliminate this feeling of being excluded by actively participating in your stepfamily's activities, decision-making, and future planning. Position yourself as an important part of your stepfamily. Contribute to family discussions, offer problem-solving solutions to dilemmas or conflicts, and above all, rejoice when good things happen; especially between your spouse and his children. Share in the love, respect, and bonding within the family. As a stepparent, decide how you *want* to fit into this stepfamily.

Stepparenting Decisions

Every stepparent has certain choices to consider. For example, do you want to be part of the discipline or leave that to your partner? These are questions that you will need to ask yourself, and remember, these are choices; not requirements. Think now of questions within your stepfamily that you have asked yourself. Do I want to participate in my stepchild's school activities? Do I want to attend plays, soccer games, or madrigal concerts? Do I want to cook for the entire family or should my stepchildren have a night when they each prepare a meal? Do I want to join the carpool and drive my stepchildren and their friends to school?

Have you made specific decisions as a stepparent within your own stepfamily? If so, what were they? Have your choices worked for you? Why or why not? Take this opportunity to evaluate one decision that you have made as a stepparent. Write down the positive or negative outcome of that choice. Did it work out the way you planned? If yes, great. If not, can you modify that decision now to make it more effective?

Sometimes we feel that the decisions we make cannot ever change. The key is to know what we can change and what we can't. For example, if early in your role as a stepparent you decided to enforce a house rule that everyone in the family had to check the chore schedule daily, that may not have been the most realistic decision you have ever made. But, interestingly, the rule has been operating for years. Someone brings it to your attention that this rule was always kind of silly and asks why we are still doing it? Can it be changed? Yes. Can all family members live with that? Yes. If you have any rules currently operating in your stepfamily that you feel simply do not work, write them down. Make notes about various ways they can be changed to improve your stepfamily. Remember that you don't necessarily have to live with things that you don't like. With communication and negotiation, stepparents can have a positive influence in the working of their stepfamily and gain a level of respect at the same time.

Another significant question that stepparents ask themselves (or should ask themselves) is, What role do I want to play in my stepchild's life? Have you thought about this question in your own stepfamily? Have you asked your partner about this? Have you asked your stepchild about this? I think you should. For stepparents, there is no law that says that we have to figure out everything. We can ask for help, and regarding this major question, sometimes the help is directly in front of us. So, if you haven't asked yourself this question yet, here is your chance. What role *do* you want to play in your stepchild's life?

To help answer this, try this exercise. Jot down a few sentences about what kind of relationship you'd like to develop with your stepchild. For example, do you want to be a friend, an acquaintance, or a confidante? How intense and involved you wish to become with your stepchild will determine what roles are available to you. Do you want to be involved in every detail of his life? How realistic is that with your own stepchild? Would you rather view from the sidelines, looking in from the outside, but not actually being in the thick of things? Basically, allowing your partner to handle it all—the good, the bad, and the ugly. Would you like to be a part-time participant in the activities? You can choose how active you wish to become in your stepchild's life. But before you begin any of these roles, a couple of things need to happen. First, you need to work through this decision with your partner, and second, find out how your stepchild feels about it.

Why would you need to work through this with your partner? Imagine this: You are a new stepparent in a new stepfamily. Your partner has been thinking about how the stepfamily will operate and he had this vision of how his new mate would minimally interact with his children. Cut to you bouncing in and completely destroying this vision, telling his kids what to do, for example, or taking over an activity that he always did before. Parents are extremely sensitive about how an outsider (that would be you) is going to relate to their children. So, check with your partner to see how he would like to see you interact with the children. Compromise is such a wonderful thing. The word should be engraved on every stepparent license.

Being a Parent Versus Being a Stepparent

How is a parent different from a stepparent? The obvious difference is that the children do not belong to the stepparent. Therefore, the stepparent may not have as strong a commitment to the children as the parent. The stepparent may have to be educated about the future plans for the stepchildren and how these will affect her role as a stepparent. For example, if the parent plans to finance his child's college education, will that mean that you will need to provide money toward that goal, or sacrifice in some other way for the stepchild? As a stepparent, are you willing to do that? These are questions that will probably surface at some point, and it's usually best to address them before you marry. A financial situation could surprise you down the road if you weren't expecting it. It's all a matter of planning and knowing ahead of time what to expect from your marriage to a parent.

Another difference between being a parent and being a stepparent is that, ultimately, the parent's opinion will dominate. That is just the way it is. As stepparents, we will not hold the position of highest authority, even though we may try to make ourselves *think* that we do. Sure, when your partner is out of town or unavailable for some reason, you will be in charge. But stepchildren always have a higher-ranking person that they can connect with if they don't like one of your decisions. Your stepchild will accept her parent's decision—so hopefully you and your partner will agree on many things!

Perhaps the most significant difference between a parent and a stepparent is unconditional love. A parent is unconditionally loved by her children; you are not. Your stepchild will always turn to his parent for that loving word, affection, or when he needs advice. If your stepparenting efforts have paid off, you may be fortunate enough that your stepchildren will come to you for these things as well. But, if you've done a good job as a stepparent and your stepchildren still don't come to you, please try not to feel rejected and left out. It's frustrating and painful, but your stepchildren may not even realize they are affecting you. It is a natural instinct for them to go to their parents for what they need.

How to Figure Out What Kind of Stepparent You Want to Be

In addition to the various stepparenting styles, there are also strategies that you, as a stepparent, have the opportunity to employ in carving out a niche for yourself in your stepfamily. What is the difference between a stepparenting style and a stepparenting strategy?

Basically, the stepparenting style is comprised of the characteristics that you want to adopt as a stepparent. For example, if you choose the superwoman/superman stepparent style, characteristics will include doing everything for everyone the best that you possibly can all the time. Wow. Good luck. A stepparenting strategy is the method by which you will put these characteristics into action. For example, if you want to be the super-stepparent, how are you going to do that and survive?

The strategy that you use to achieve the stepparent style that you want will be completely determined by the type of stepparent you are planning to emulate. Or, your strategy will determine your style. First, we will need to identify the strategies that you may want to consider. The strategy you choose will largely be dependent upon the kind of person you are. For example, if you are an assertive person, the strategy you use to implement your stepparenting style will be quite different than if you are a more laid-back person, more inclined to let things happen.

Take a minute and mentally describe yourself. What characteristics would you say best describe how you try to talk to someone about a new idea? Now write down those characteristics, as you'll need to refer back to them from time to time. First, how would you implement a new idea at work? Or how would you introduce a new idea to a friend? The answer to this question will describe your process of identifying how you strategically approach a concept. Second, are you comfortable with how you approach this? Suppose you are an assertive person. As an assertive person, do you initiate the conversation about presenting a new idea to someone? Probably. After initiating this idea, do you then also offer suggestions to improve on this idea? Probably. But, if you are nonassertive, your approach may be much different. As a nonassertive person, you may wait for someone else to suggest an idea. Once heard, you may add suggestions later. Or, perhaps you have a completely different approach. And if you are not satisfied with the way you present new information, here is your opportunity to change that.

First, you need to decide on a strategy, such as will you be direct with your stepchildren or fade into the background. Please write that down now. You must be sure that you can live with this strategy. For example, if you are assertive and suggest ideas, you may endure some criticism. You must be prepared to live with that; try not to be defensive about it. You need to be comfortable with taking some criticism from your stepfamily members. If you have chosen to be nonassertive about it, your stepfamily may tell you how they want you to stepparent. Can you live with that? Now that you know your strategy, let's go through some steps for how to introduce your stepparenting style to your stepfamily.

Suppose that you have chosen to be the superman/superwoman stepparent. You could begin doing everything for everyone. That may work, but guess what—members of your stepfamily will grow accustomed to having you do everything. Eventually, they will take you for granted and stop appreciating what you do for them. Gather your stepfamily members together; if you have dinner together, discuss your concerns at the table. Begin by sharing that you have been thinking about what kind of stepparent you want to be. Be prepared for absolute silence. Either they will be shocked that you are putting this much thought into it, or the stepchildren will appreciate that you are telling them ahead of time, so they don't have to wait to see what you are going to be like on a day-to-day basis. Once you've introduced the topic, because you are assertive and want to discuss and resolve this issue, continue with telling them the type of stepparent you'd like to be. Let's start with an example of dialogue between you and your stepchild.

You: I've been thinking about this stepparenting thing, and I've decided on what kind of stepparent I want to be in this stepfamily.

Stepchild: Really?

You: Yeah, well, I thought it might be best if we talked about it up front so there are no surprises down the road for either one of us.

Stepchild: Sounds good to me. What kind of stepparent do you want to be?

You: Basically I want to be there for you as your stepparent, and try to help you in any way that I can.

Stepchild: Wow, that sounds great.

You: I'm glad you think so, but actually doing it might not be as easy as wanting to do it. So, I'll need your help in trying to be the stepparent that works for both of us.

Stepchild: I like that idea, and I'll help if I can.

This conversation will open the door for your stepchild to think about not only what kind of stepparent you want to be, but just maybe she will begin thinking about how important her role as the stepchild will be, too. At the very least, your stepchild will know that you have cared enough to include her in your decision. If your child is not readily receptive to a verbal explanation, she may need to see the type of stepparent you will be. You may need to show her what type of stepparent you will be.

Ronald had been a stepparent for only a short time but had already discovered that things weren't working as smoothly in his stepfamily as he would have liked. He was experiencing difficulty with his stepchildren because they were not following his instructions. Ronald felt the stepchildren should listen when he spoke and that when he told them to do something, they should do it. He felt this was a direct way to handle his stepchildren, and he was genuinely confused about the responses he received from them.

As we explored this issue, we first discussed Ronald's impression of a stepparent's role. His wife came into the marriage with the children, he said, and he expected that, as their stepfather, he would participate in the discipline in the household. Ronald and his wife had not discussed this issue before their marriage. Ronald indicated that it had not occurred to them that they *should* talk about this. As the story unfurled, it was also clear that Ronald and his wife had not discussed his directness and that her children were not used to this type of personality.

An additional complication was that Ronald was unsure of what kind of stepparent he was going to be. His wife, Rhoda, was a bit more laid-back, and the children were accustomed to this style of parenting. His aggressive personality was new and confusing to the children. The children's routines were established prior to Ronald's arrival in the stepfamily, and both Rhoda and Ronald had not considered the possibility of a clash between a different style of parenting and the stepparenting model. Interestingly, Rhoda seemed equally surprised as it became clear that their styles conflicted, and that was probably the reason Ronald felt ineffective with the stepchildren.

Rhoda and I began exploring how a parent can assist the stepparent in interacting with her children, particularly talking with her children first to pave the way for the introduction of another adult—someone who will actively participate in their daily lives—then discussing the issue as a family. It is important that the stepchildren have access to this information and be encouraged to ask questions of just what a stepparent has in mind. It is equally important that, as the stepparent, you ask your stepchildren for their input and help. This gives the stepchildren permission to feel included, to take an active role in the daily workings of the stepfamily. It is an essential tool in building a bond with your stepchild.

Selecting Stepparenting Styles with the Stepfamily

I have already discussed stepparenting styles and a strategy for introducing those styles. The case history above illustrated the importance of allowing your stepchild to have input into the stepparenting style that you choose and the strategy that you use to implement it. Why? Input from your stepchild will help validate the strategy you want to adopt. For example, at work, suppose you have a new boss, and there is much apprehension about this new boss—what kind of person will she be? what style of management does she use? will she be fair, or will she be a tyrant? All of these things run through anyone's mind when a new supervisory figure enters their life.

It's similar in the stepfamily between stepparents and stepchildren. The stepchildren are definitely wondering what kind of person you are and, particularly, how they should interact with you. This is an opportunity to clear the air and give your stepchild a break at the same time. As you discuss with your stepchild the type of stepparent you want to be, as well as your strategy or how you will approach this, you will answer his questions and probably be able to see a visible sign of relief! Stepchildren are concerned about this issue. They don't know you as well as their parent, and they will not know what to expect from you. They do expect consistency from their parents and will probably expect the same from you. So, what better way to offer relief to them and to you than by discussing it *before* you run into obstacles.

Your stepchild can offer valuable input for you. How? She's been through this with parents. She knows what works in her house and what probably won't. So it would be most beneficial for you to know your spouse's parenting style. You do not need to adopt your partner's exact style because a stepparent doesn't necessarily parent exactly like his partner. However, you can mesh your two different styles to make it less confusing for your stepchild. And when you solicit input from your stepchild, you will only improve your family's situation.

For example, if your stepchild is accustomed to a more laid-back style of parenting, and you come barreling in demanding this or that, you may encounter problems. You want to have a successful interaction with your stepchild, whether it's in a situation of praise or discipline. So, begin by asking your stepchild about her parent's style. This is a great question to start with for a couple of reasons. It's helpful to listen to your stepchild describe how she has been parented so that you can understand how your stepchild perceives the situation. You will also know what your stepchild will respond to, obey, and follow (hopefully without question).

One terrific benefit to this method is that your stepchildren will be happily surprised that you are considering their feelings—because their parents are not required to *discuss* their parenting style. As the stepparent, you are. You are not their parent, yet you are taking on a role, in this case, possibly as disciplinarian, to people who are not your children. Think of the awesome level of that task. Your stepchildren's opinion can be a great asset to you in knowing how you should proceed. Your stepchildren can give you insight to their own behavior system—what they'll respond to and what they won't. Listen to them, and take what you need from their conversation to help you in your role as a stepparent.

Sometimes stepparents feel that their stepchild's opinion is irrelevant. That type of attitude concerns me. By discussing your stepparenting style with your stepchildren and soliciting their opinion, you are not asking them to *tell* you how to parent. You are looking for information to *add to or enhance* what you already know you are going to do, to make it work. It is paramount that a stepparent understand this. It's also essential that you express this carefully so that your stepchildren do not think you are asking them how to parent themselves. That's not what we are trying to accomplish here. Your role is to acknowledge your stepchildren's position in all of this; what parenting style they are used to and what changes they can accommodate. Let's examine a dialogue about this issue.

You: We were talking earlier about the kind of stepparent that I want to be to you, and I'm curious about a couple of things. Your Mom (or Dad) seems to talk to you easily when she approaches you about stuff, whether it's good or bad. Have you ever thought about how she discusses things with you?

Stepchild: No, I just listen when she talks.

You: Well, like the other night, when she was talking with you about your report card, it seemed that your Mom just gently asked you about your grades and you both started talking about it.

Stepchild: I thought she was really going to yell at me for that C+ in Math.

You: Most kids would probably feel that way, but your Mom doesn't really yell at you. At least not that I have heard.

Stepchild: No, she doesn't, I just say that sometimes. Actually, Mom is really good when she wants to talk about something. She doesn't get mad or go hysterical on me or anything. I really like that.

You: Yeah, and it's great that you do what she asks of you.

Stepchild: It's easy to do stuff for Mom. I know she appreci-
ates it.

You: How do you know?

Stepchild: She'll tell me or hug me or something. And I just
know.

This is your cue! Your stepchild has just given you the pro-
tocol of how the parenting process has been successful in this
family so far. Now it's up to you to take that information and
mold it into your style and strategy.

Once you've opened the door to accessing this information,
you can proceed to talking with your stepchild about the approach that you plan to use. If you are more assertive than your
partner, explain that to your stepchild. Ask him if he understands. Ask him if he can work with you on that. Pose a question
such as, "Do you want to be told to clean your room or would
you rather I ask you?" Remember, you are the adult here, and
you are not asking your stepchild to determine *how* you will
stepparent. You've already decided that in your style, whether
it's the superstepparent, the disengaged, the uncertain, or the
friendly. At this juncture, you are asking your stepchild to help
you decide what strategy will work. Your approach is crucial; it
can be the deciding factor between successful and unsuccessful
stepparenting. You can be any style of stepparent you like, but
how your stepchild responds to you and interacts with you will
determine how well your style is working.

Should I Compromise with My Stepchild on Strategy?

Yes. Why? Because you may have the most perfected approach or strategy in your stepparenting style, but it will not be workable unless your stepchild is receptive to it. Your stepchild has been raised by parents that used a parenting style that she grew accustomed to and could predict to some degree. Your stepchild already responds to a familiar and, perhaps, comfortable parenting style.

Enter you. You come waltzing into this stepfamily and think that you are going to be the perfect stepparent. Good. Right about then, you tell your stepchild that you don't like something he did; he is completely surprised by your approach, and he walks. You didn't get what you needed (a response) and your stepchild didn't get what he was looking for (an understanding stranger). As the stepparent, you analyze this incident for minutes, hours, maybe days. We want to do the right thing and we want our stepchildren to like us, so we tend to focus on what went wrong. Dwelling on it by ourselves might not be the answer. Instead, discuss it with your stepchild; preferably *before* an incident like the above takes place.

As the adult in the situation, it may be easier for you to adapt to the stepparenting situation. First, find out what parenting style your stepchild responds to. Second, modify your style and strategy to that parenting style, and build on it. Add some mentoring, guidance, and direction to what your stepchild has already received from her parent. Be an asset to your stepchild.

This will bond you and your stepchild in what could otherwise be an extremely sensitive situation.

Look at it this way. As a child, would you have wanted some outsider to discipline you in a way that you disliked immediately? Think about how your stepchild feels. Not only has one parent been removed from his living environment, but now he must contend with another adult that he does not love unconditionally. Imagine what that must be like for your stepchild. It can be extremely confusing. It can be equally confusing for you as the stepparent, but in a different way. You may not know what type of stepparent you want to be, and you may not know how to approach your stepchild. This is your chance to make it work the first time. Talk with your stepchild. Ask him questions. Give him an opportunity to ask you questions. If you don't agree, compromise with your stepchild. Come to an agreement on how he will respond to you. When you actually apply what you have agreed to, you may need to remind your stepchild of what he agreed to; kids are still kids. It may even help to write up a contract. The following is an example of such a contract:

Contract between stepparent and stepchild (use names)

1. Kendra (stepchild) must clean her room once per week. If Kendra does not clean her room by Saturday, Louise (stepparent) will *ask* Kendra to clean her room by Saturday at 5:00 P.M. Kendra will not respond angrily to Louise's request.

2. Kendra will help prepare dinner on Wednesdays. Louise will help Kendra decide what the meal will be and help her with the grocery shopping.

If any of the above situations are not followed according to this contract, Louise will be responsible for disciplining Kendra. Kendra will not be allowed to have friends over on the weekend or her homework must be done at the kitchen table for one hour every night for a week (or whatever method you use).

_____   _____

Kendra   *Louise*

The stepparent's job in a contract is to monitor that contract and follow up to be sure the agreements are kept. This is an example of a simple contract that stepparents have prepared with their stepchildren. The purpose is to clarify what will happen beforehand so that both parties understand how the task will take place in the household. The contract also acts as a reminder to your stepchild of the chores she is asked to fulfill. Kids tend to respond to a contract. It gives them a sense of responsibility and seriousness. A contract like this is only effective, though, if you follow it. It is your responsibility as the stepparent to follow up. Also this contract can be modified at any time. Once the behavior or task is understood and your stepchild is able to complete it without constant reminding, you can cross it off the list and add another if you like. This will also give your stepchild a clear picture of how you plan to stepparent, and she will know, with or without a contract, what to expect from you.

Be Prepared to Modify Your Stepparenting Style

Through the years, you will probably experience different stepparenting styles and strategies. As your stepchildren grow and mature, they will need less stepparenting or different stepparenting. It is important that you recognize this yet still maintain consistency in your stepparenting while modifying your style. Your stepchild will appreciate that you have recognized his maturity. And at age sixteen, he may not need to be reminded continually of his chores (he might, but let's be hopeful). We want to build a lasting trust between you and your stepchild, and being able to adapt to his growth and development will be a giant step toward bonding.

One drawback for you, as the stepparent, may be that you became so adjusted to using one style, it may be difficult for you to change! This is a common challenge for any parent. Change is difficult; but when it comes to bonding with your stepchildren, you will need to be able to change as they change. Younger stepchildren bond differently than adolescents, and adolescents bond differently than adult stepchildren. You will have the opportunity to bond with your stepchild through many stages. What an extraordinary experience. So, as the adult, you must recognize and adjust your style to the changing stages that your stepchildren pass through, so that you can continue to bond and grow with them.

How to Work Through the Confusion of this Adjustment

You may wonder how you will be able to recognize when your stepchild is ready for change. This may stir up something in your stomach that feels like fear. Relax. Your stepchild will help you with this. For example, if you still deal with your fifteen-year-old stepchild as if she is eight years old, she'll probably inform you. Stepchildren may not hesitate to point out the obvious things that you may have missed! Look at this in a positive way. She is only trying to assert that she is growing and maturing. As you are closer to an equal and adult relationship with your stepchild, you will be able to see the effects of all of your hard work over the years as a stepparent.

How You Are Evaluated As a Stepparent

That's right, you are evaluated as a stepparent. Can you believe it? So you've chosen a stepparenting style that works for you, and you've worked out what strategy works best to implement the style. Now you wait to see how you did.

Who will evaluate your stepparenting? Probably everyone in the extended family that has a chance to observe you with your stepchild. But on the more immediate front, your partner, your stepchildren, and you will be evaluating you. Your partner's evaluation may be more obvious to you with regular discussions about how things are working for you as a stepparent. But your stepchildren's evaluation of you may be more hidden. And finally, you should also evaluate yourself, knowing where to change things when necessary to improve your performance.

Your spouse will evaluate your performance as a stepparent for specific reasons. He will want to monitor how his child reacts to you as a stepparent. Your partner will be concerned if his child feels criticized or demeaned in any way. But your partner should pay attention to any positives developing between you and your stepchildren. This is equally important. As you build a bond with your stepchildren, it is critical that your partner actively *help* you build that bond. Without your partner's help and encouragement with his child, it can be difficult to build a bond with your stepchild. Your partner should describe to you what he sees as positive between you and your stepchild, but he should also point out any possible negatives. When your partner critiques your stepparenting, try to absorb this information without feeling defensive. Please accept this information as helpful, and as a way to examine your stepparenting style to see how you can improve. This feedback will be invaluable to you, particularly if your stepchild doesn't give you any signals that what you are doing isn't working. And if your partner is not offering you constructive criticism, please tell him that you need this and *ask for a critique*. It's difficult to be a successful stepparent all on your own. You need help from those you live with everyday.

Your stepchildren should also be evaluating you, and, believe me, they probably are. But you may not know it! It's doubtful that they will openly tell you that you are doing a great job. It's also not likely that they will come right out and tell you that you are doing a lousy job. In fact, you may not hear any feedback from your stepchildren, but it's highly probable that they have formed an opinion of you as a stepparent. Aren't you dying to find out what that opinion is? Your stepchildren will be evaluating you as a stepparent for different reasons than your partner. Your stepchildren will be concerned with how much freedom you allow them in your style as well as your approach with them—do you yell (a favorite teen term) at them or talk with them in a tone they don't fear? Your stepchildren will also be preoccupied with your behavior around their friends. Finally, they will wonder what topics they can talk with you about and what topics are off limits. For example, can they talk with you about their other parent without you going ballistic? Keep a close eye on these types of interactions with your stepchild, and you should pass the evaluation with ease.

Finally, you should be continually evaluating yourself as a stepparent. When you evaluate yourself, it is important to consider how you feel in your new role. Does it feel comfortable? Does it feel like you? If not, I would suggest some adaptation toward a style that feels comfortable and workable. You are going to be in this role for a long time. It is essential that you feel you can live with it day to day. Also, if you feel like a tyrant and that's simply not you, do some re-evaluation. Or if you feel that you are too soft in certain areas, again, re-examine the style and strategy that you've chosen. Continue to modify until you get it right—where it works for your partner, your stepchildren, and you.

5

STEP FIVE

When Having a Stepfamily
Wasn't Your Idea

"When I met my wife, I wasn't even looking for a relationship, but I guess sometimes that's how you meet that special person. We fell in love, got married, and I found myself not only in a relationship but in a family. I knew she had four kids, but I guess I thought it would be mostly just the two of us after we were married. Now it's my wife, me, and four kids!"

Why is it that when you meet someone, you don't always see everything that comes with this wonderful person, particularly if this person is a parent? A fantasy plays out in your mind like a movie. You and your new spouse will have all your time alone together and enjoy being with each other every minute. Yes, he has children, but the children will be well-behaved, and there won't be any problems in your perfect stepfamily. Cut. Rewind. This may be how the movie would go, but it isn't real life.

You will enjoy a honeymoon stage in your new stepfamily.

Everyone, including you, will be on their best behavior for a while. You might think that being a stepparent is the most wonderful job in the world. But you may be in for a reality check once the honeymoon is over. Maybe you're wondering how to tell when the honeymoon *is* over. You won't have any problem identifying when this occurs. Trust me. Some tips that the honeymoon is over include arguments, more conflict in the home, and true personalities presenting themselves—including yours.

If you suddenly feel like your new family situation is not what you envisioned, you are not alone. Many people who enter a relationship with a spouse who is already a parent are well aware that they will have to adjust to having children. But for one reason or another, when the actual cohabitation begins, the children become more real and lifelike. Reality has set in, and it can be completely different than what you allowed yourself to imagine. It can be a real shock when it finally does hit. In a stepfamily, illusions disappear quickly after moving in together. When you come home that first night after work, rush into the house and the waiting arms of your new spouse, you may also be rushing into the arms of stepchildren! Some people have difficulty with this, and understandably so. Entering into a relationship still represents visions of a one-on-one with your loved one, the intimacy of just the two of you, and the togetherness that cohabitation brings. This is true in most relationships. In a stepfamily, this may also be true, but with an added bonus of two or three or four—stepchildren, that is! If you are experiencing difficulty with adjusting to not only your new spouse but also her children, don't despair. There are some things that you can do to ensure a smooth transition.

When the Reality of Living Together Sinks In

Ground rules. If you have ever been in a sports activity—volleyball, football, tennis, squash—then you know there are ground rules. Think of your new stepfamily as a sports activity. Before you begin, you need to determine the rules of the game for all of the positions. The good news is that you and your spouse are the team captains. The bad news is that sometimes the captains have the toughest job.

First, you need to understand the change from what you had before to the transition of reality. As mentioned earlier, members of the stepfamily are on their best behavior initially. No one wants to deliberately hurt another person in the household while getting to know each other or to have a bad impression of them right from the start. So, everyone may pretend to be in a good mood to avoid any negativity because they don't know what will happen if they do create conflict. *What will Mom say if I start an argument with Ted, her new husband and my new stepfather? What will my new wife, Emily, say if I have a disagreement with her son, Andy?*

These kinds of questions dominate our thoughts early on. After a while, however, the acting gets old, and we begin to be ourselves. Why? Because most of us get irritated by others we live with from time to time. *So what if Emily is upset that Andy and I fight and argue? I feel strongly about this particular issue*

121

and I won't give in. I don't care what Mom thinks if Ted and I get into it. I'm tired of dancing around it. Although it is perfectly normal, watch for sudden or gradual change, and acknowledge it when it occurs. Point it out to others in the stepfamily. Once it is out in the open, it can be discussed and addressed.

Some of you may enjoy the honeymoon period for a long time. But disappointment sometimes accompanies the end of this honeymoon period, and it can help to discuss this disillusion in an attempt to help everyone in the family move on. Why is this change so disappointing? The primary reason is that it opens the door to conflict, and many people have difficulty with conflict, especially stepparents. Dealing with conflict is never easy. Think of your own family. Have you experienced conflict with them? Many of us have family members that we love unconditionally but with whom we still argue. And if we have trouble resolving something with someone we love unconditionally, imagine how difficult this same process would be with a stepchild. So you may experience disappointment, but it will be easier if you are prepared.

DEALING WITH DISAPPOINTMENT

There will be certain conditions that you may need to accept. You are living with other people who are not perfect; that includes you. At some point, it is inevitable that someone in your stepfamily will do something that will annoy you. You may also unintentionally irritate someone in your stepfamily. Accept it. Develop ways to deal with it that work for you, and move on. As a stepparent, you have a choice. You can choose to see this change as a disappointment, or you can choose to see it as an opportunity. Being a member of a stepfamily is a special experience. It is a gift that has been given to you. Use it wisely and make it your goal, as the stepparent, to try to be understanding, encouraging, and easy to work with, and these characteristics will make you a strong and respected member of your stepfamily.

Once reality does set in, what happens to the visions of romance and the life you had planned that didn't include the children every moment? Hold on, here comes another one of those situations stepparents must learn to live with and handle with diplomacy.

When You Want Romantic Time Alone, and Your Spouse Wants to Include the Children

Have you ever sat at your office desk and fantasized about this new partner that you just married? Have you daydreamed about all of the things you want to do together—maybe travel, attend local social events, or take on activities at home, such as gardening or exercising, whatever you and your spouse like to do that attracted you to each other in the first place? Most people do fantasize about their partner and how they see their life together. With stepparents, these fantasies do not always include the stepchild. Why? Because they are not used to including children and they simply forget; parents need to understand this. Sometimes parents feel that stepparents deliberately exclude the children when they want to do something together. With some stepparents, it may be deliberate. I would guess, however, that most of the time it is an innocent mistake, and not something that a stepparent deviously planned. People have a tendency to think the worst, as you have probably experienced. So, it is essential to clarify to your spouse that you do not want to exclude the children. You may need help remembering that there *are* children involved now, and that will change the way you do things and see things.

It is important for you to ground yourself in the reality of being a stepparent. What does that mean? Ask yourself this: Do you really know what it means to be a stepparent? It took me a long time to understand this particular piece of the puzzle. And other stepparents have expressed the same admission. As a stepparent, you may think that you know exactly what that title means. And, if so, great. If not, let's review some of the more sensitive points of stepparenthood. Part of being a stepparent means that you may not be able to have your new partner all to yourself all of the time. There. It's said. It's out there. Now you may be saying, "Well, of course, I knew that." But the first time a situation occurs where you are going out to dinner (or wherever), and you're thinking it's going to be just you and your partner, and then at the last minute, you find out the stepchild is coming, too, the surprise can sometimes trigger resentment, anger, and confusion. Why? What if you had something special planned for that evening, either to do with your partner or to tell your partner something special, alone, in a private one-on-one? Please, for your sake, learn and accept now that this can and will happen. Also, figure out right now how you are going to react. If you determine now what your reaction will be and practice it ahead of time in your mind, you have a better chance of not blowing it when this "surprise" actually occurs. Your partner will include your stepchildren in things—and your partner may be so used to including his children that he may forget to tell you! Remember, be an adaptable stepparent. Cooperate. Cooperate. Cooperate.

Someone once asked why romance and togetherness aren't always present in a stepfamily. Well, are they always present in a traditional family? Probably not. It depends upon the players involved. If you are a stepparent who can handle unexpected occurrences (that you might not like) and accept that you may not be informed of what's going on all the time, you may have a decent shot at more romance and togetherness with your partner. But this is a difficult role, and I caution you about how you plan to handle it. Not everyone is capable of being the one who needs to adjust *every* time, and that is not what I am suggesting. Each stepfamily member has a responsibility to be flexible and to make adjustments with certain situations. The stepparent cannot be expected to compromise each time. As a stepparent, you are also entitled to moments alone with your spouse that do not include the stepchildren. But, likewise, the other members of your stepfamily are equally entitled to their times together that do not include you. Remember, they were a family before you came along; there is a history there and a way of doing things that may be different from what you expect.

THE BENEFITS OF INCLUDING YOUR STEPCHILDREN

It is quite normal for your partner to want to include her children in activities. And, as a stepparent, I know that you know that. In order to understand this, let's first look at how activities with your stepchildren can help the stepfamily. This will strengthen you as a family unit. Doing things together will allow each of you to get to know one another, particularly the stepparent and stepchild. It is a great way to initiate bonding as well as to maintain the bond once established. Stepchildren are often quite insightful and perceptive, and including them can be an entertaining and educating experience for you as a stepparent. It would also be an invaluable experience for you to observe how your partner interacts with his children, providing insight into a relationship that should be important to you. Spending time with your stepchildren can be a fun, rewarding experience, broadening your social networking within the family. And, finally, it will help strengthen the intimacy between you and your partner by demonstrating your acceptance of the stepchild.

THE DANGER OF INCLUDING THE STEPCHILDREN

Just as there are positives, there are also negatives. Including the stepchild in too many activities can also place the adult relationship at risk. How? This may give your stepchild the message that, as adults, you do not need time alone. The stepchild may take for granted that she will be included in all adult activities. Clearly, the adult relationship, as any other relationship, needs time to develop and grow. You and your partner will need separate time together to build the foundation of your marriage. The adult relationship may also be at risk when you include the stepchild at all times because the stepparent may become annoyed or frustrated that his spouse wants the children along each and every time. This is understandable. The parent in this relationship must understand the stepparent's need for space from the children. The stepparent has the right to want time alone with his partner, without the children. This is crucial to the success of the adult relationship, which is the core of the stepfamily.

When It Is Okay to Object to Including Your Stepchild

As a stepparent, you may feel uncomfortable about asking your partner to not include her children in an activity. We've all been there. This is clearly a sensitive situation and must be handled delicately and with diplomacy. First, figure out why you don't want to invite your stepchild. Do you have a legitimate reason for why you'd rather do this activity alone with your partner? Do you and your partner need to be alone on this one? Is it selfish? You should ask and answer these questions before you begin a dialogue with your partner on this issue. We all want time alone with our partners, and if there is a reasonable explanation for not including the stepchild, your partner has an obligation to listen and try to understand.

How do you ask your partner to exclude his child in an activity? Suppose you have an event where you might not want to invite your stepchild, and you need to talk with your partner about it. It's a sensitive issue so a sensitive conversation is required, as in the example below:

You: Honey, you know we have that trip planned for next week.

Partner: Yes, and I can't wait. I thought we'd take the kids and we could pack a picnic lunch.

You: Yeah, that sounds fun. We've taken the kids on lots of outings like this, and we've had some good times. But what would you think if, this time, just the two of us went on this trip? It could be a nice getaway for us and we could spend some time together alone, and feel like a couple for a while.

Partner: Oh, I don't know. The kids really look forward to these trips and I wouldn't want to disappoint them.

You: I sure wouldn't want to disappoint them, either, but we've taken them many times before. I'm feeling the need to spend time alone with you. After all, it's been quite some time since we've done that, and I miss the two of us being alone together. Maybe we could start planning some activities for just ourselves, so that the kids won't expect to go with us each time. That way they won't be disappointed and we won't need to feel guilty about not taking them. How do you feel about that?

Partner: Well, if we take it slow and plan ahead, it might just work. I would like some time alone with you, too, and I know the kids can be a lot of work at times to entertain. Alright, let's try it.

The key here is for your partner to feel comfortable with not having the children along on each and every activity. She may immediately disagree with you because she feels guilty. You must approach this situation with an open mind, and possibly a good deal of patience. Allow your partner to grow accustomed to the idea of not including the children. Seek a balance; include the children at certain times to meet your partner's needs, and negotiate for time alone to meet your needs. But don't think that you can have it your way each time. That is not reasonable and it is not fair to your partner or to the stepchild. Practice compromise.

Times will come when you will have to accept that your stepchild will be included in your activities, such as with family get-togethers, family vacations, and other routine events in your stepfamily. Most important, you and your partner should agree on when the stepchild will or won't be included, and your partner must feel comfortable with the decision. After all, it is his child, but he also has a responsibility to you, his partner, in the adult relationship.

Mona was a new stepparent who was having difficulty with her husband over the issue of including the children in activities. Mona did not have children, and her husband, Dwight, had two children, both girls. Dwight and Mona had only been married a short time before this issue surfaced. Mona described the situation as very difficult because Dwight appeared to feel that the children should be with them virtually everywhere they went. At first, Mona accepted this, thinking that Dwight was working to build the stepfamily. Dwight even included the children when he and Mona went out to dinner.

After a while, Mona became agitated when Dwight continued to include the children, even on what she felt should have been intimate dinners. She felt that the children were being forced upon her and that this was unfair. Mona approached Dwight with the idea that maybe they could spend some time alone, and according to Mona, Dwight would not even listen to her. He became immediately defensive and accused Mona of not liking his kids. Unpleasant as that may be, it often happens in stepfamilies. Parents are extremely sensitive to their children's feelings, and sometimes any perception of rejection may cause the parent to react this way. Mona was now even more hurt because of Dwight's accusation.

Mona clearly had some work ahead of her. She knew that Dwight had always been a reasonable person, and therefore she needed to appeal to his sense of reason for negotiation. Mona and Dwight struggled with this issue for a very long time, often needing therapeutic intervention. But the final results were positive. It was discovered that Dwight felt that if he did not include his children in each and every activity, the children would feel neglected or unwanted; a common feeling among stepchildren. Once Mona was aware of how Dwight felt, they were on equal negotiating ground. It took time and much discussion, but eventually Dwight reached the acceptance stage at which he knew that he had a responsibility to Mona but also realized that what Mona was asking for was not unreasonable. One of the obstacles in this situation was that Dwight did not feel he could explain things thoroughly enough for the children to understand. Mona and Dwight received information on how to talk with the children so that the children would not feel neglected or unwanted. It was a slow process, but once this was achieved, the situation worked out in a balance that proved enjoyable for everyone. Mona had more time with Dwight, and Dwight developed a closer bond with his own children.

Both you and your partner will have a different rationale for including the children in activities at different times. Knowing this will be a big step toward compromise. As with other steps in this book, discussing this before you live together as a family is essential. Why? Because, just like Dwight in the case study above, your partner may feel resentful if she feels you don't want to include the stepchildren every time. Parents often feel that their children have suffered enough hurt and rejection that there is not room for any more. This is true—to a certain extent. But it's not reality. Stepchildren have been hurt because their parents are no longer together, for whatever reason. And certainly, as stepparents, we do not want to cause rejection in any way. But there is a huge difference between rejection and not wanting to include the children in every activity. If the two are seen as the same, that's a problem. Your partner must understand that not including the children once in a while is *not* rejecting them. Quite the contrary. It is a way of demonstrating to the children that you and your partner love each other and want to spend time alone together.

Stepchildren want to see their parents happy, and if that means being alone with their new partner, then they are usually supportive. Sometimes parents are not able to read their children correctly—in a divorce situation this is quite understandable. With all of the emotions flying around, it's difficult to pinpoint exactly where the children are with regard to everything. And sometimes divorced parents feel that they must spend all of their time with their children, after the divorce, to ensure that the children know they can count on their parents to be there. This is reasonable and understandable. But my experience has been that stepchildren are usually happy to see their parent find a partner and will want to work with the parent to make this new relationship succeed. Remember, I used the word "usually"—I realize that this isn't always the case.

WHEN YOU CAN'T AGREE, YOU MAY NEED TO ADJUST

But what happens if you and your partner absolutely cannot arrive at an agreement on this issue? There are ways to work this out, but they may require more adjustment on the part of the stepparent. It is critical that the stepparent understands how his or her partner feels. This is probably one of the most sensitive situations you will be exposed to in your stepfamily. If you have a partner who insists on including the children at all times or most of the time, but you feel differently, it will require a huge amount of maturity and sensitivity to work through this.

First, you need to find out why the parent feels so strongly about including the children. Most of the time, it is for the reason mentioned above; the parent needs to feel secure that her children know, beyond a shadow of a doubt, that she is there for them. Good. Now, based on that information, what can you do to *help* ensure that this will happen? You can be there for the stepchildren, either physically or emotionally. If you also show the stepchildren that, as their stepparent, you are there for them when they need you, two things can happen. One, you have further helped to build a bond with your stepchildren. Second, and perhaps more important on this particular issue, you will demonstrate to your partner that you, too, want the same security for the children. Once your partner feels sure that you are not excluding the children on purpose, or because you simply do not want them around, then your partner can feel safe and trust that you care for her children. This will begin to ease your partner's fears about the children feeling left out or unwanted.

Keep in mind that this process can take a long time. You are facing cement walls of emotion that have been built within your partner before you even met him. So, please, tread softly, and above all, be sensitive, understanding, and respectful of your partner, the person you love with all your energy. By working through this, your reward will be a stepfamily built on trust and caring. Always remember that your partner and stepchildren need to feel safe with you—and that, my friend, must be earned. And, of course, dealing with this issue early in the relationship will pave the way to establishing a foundation with your partner and with the children in developing and maintaining a long-term, stable family relationship. A key reward will be that your intimate relationship with your partner will be strengthened, and that will provide the basis for longevity in your relationship.

Stepparent, Another Name for Outsider

In this new family, one of the key issues becomes the stepparent's status as the outsider. You, as the stepparent, are an outsider, and how you approach and deal with your stepfamily conflicts may well determine just how long you carry this label.

What happens when an outside person comes into the family, and family routines are already established? Try to think of this as a workplace. You are hired for a new position and are all excited because of the new challenges and opportunities opening up for you. On your first day, you are given the employee handbook and personnel policies. As you begin to read, your excitement level decreases slightly because you've just read about a policy that you do not agree with. What do you do? New job, new company, guess what: You conform and do what they tell you to do, right? Then, you read on and there are a few more policies that may shock you, make you sick, or even anger you. In any event, there are policies that you simply do not agree with, but you didn't know about these policies until you read the manual. Why? Because when offered a new job, you don't always read the entire policy manual before you say yes, so you run into a few surprises. This can happen in a stepfamily, too. There are policies or routines already in place when you accept this assignment, and you don't ask to see the "family manual" before you fall in love and boom—you're in a stepfamily. So, then a few surprises come along that you don't like or agree with, and suddenly conflict erupts.

First of all, is there any way to prevent this from happening? The answer is yes. How? Ask for the family manual ahead of time. Talk to your partner about how things are done with the children—what are the holiday traditions? how does the extended family thing work? what is the routine with the other parent? You get the idea. Better yet, if you have the opportunity to observe the routines, you'll be one step ahead of this issue. If you spend time with your partner at her home prior to living together, take advantage of this time to monitor the interaction between your soon-to-be spouse and her children. Observe what roles are already established. A word of caution, however. You may encounter something that you feel you would handle differently. Make a mental note to discuss that with your partner later, not in front of the children. Once you've had an opportunity to talk about it with your partner, you may then work out a plan together before talking with the kids. You won't want to be the new kid coming in and telling everybody what to do. That usually doesn't work in the workplace, and probably won't work really well in your stepfamily, either. Any changes that you feel need to take place are not only your decision to make. You are in a stepfamily, and that means you now have partners to consult with on issues of conflict.

Margot and Brett met when they were in their early 40s. Margot had two children from a previous marriage. Brett had no children and had not been married before. Brett had been single for a long time and had established his own, comfortable lifestyle. When he met Margot, he states he was "so enamored with her that I didn't see anything else," such as the fact that she had two children who would live with them when they married.

Margot and Brett went through quite an adjustment period. Margot's children were seven and nine, and Brett now admits that he had no idea what he was getting himself into. He had no clue what the needs of a nine- and seven-year-old were, and the demands that were placed on Margot, he simply found overwhelming. Household routines were established prior to the marriage in both Brett and Margot's homes, and their task was to merge these routines into a functioning household.

There were many changes that had to be made, and weekends were a priority. Margot's children lived with her and saw their father only during the week. On weekends, the children lived with Margot and Brett. Brett was used to having his weekends alone, free to do whatever he wanted. When he married Margot, this changed drastically. Brett, of course, wanted to spend weekends with Margot, but Margot's time was reserved for the children. This became a source of discontent soon into the marriage, and Margot and Brett needed to find some neutral ground where they could begin to work through this. First of all, they examined several different options. For example, Margot considered making different visitation arrangements with her ex-spouse, so that the children might spend some weekends with their father. Another option was to have Brett rearrange his work schedule, to work more on the weekend and less in the evenings during the week in order to spend more time with Margot. They also thought about having the children stay with Margot's family members a little more often. Both Brett and Margot were willing to consider alternatives to make this work. Every stepfamily is unique, and different options may exist in each. Margot and Brett were able to successfully negotiate altered visitation arrangements so that everyone, including the children, felt comfortable.

But just as Margot was willing to change her previous way of life out of respect for Brett, he also needed to do some adjusting to the new stepfamily way of life. In particular, Brett needed to get used to the routine at dinner. Before they were married, Brett often ate out during the week and had take-out on the weekends. Now, he lived in a stepfamily that added three more people to the mix. Eating out and take-out worked okay some of the time, but, clearly, it was necessary to make some adjustment for the stepchildren, and that meant cooking at home more often. Margot had started doing much of the meal preparation for the stepfamily but soon found, with working and taking care of the kids, that this was time consuming, a situation faced by many parents. Brett needed to accept some cooking responsibility. In this case, that meant learning how to cook basic meals. He was aware that he needed to change his own routine.

The key to success in this stepfamily was certainly the willingness on the part of both adults to recognize that they needed to change, and to respect each other in making adjustments to make this work. Routines can always be altered; showing willingness and respect for the other members of the family cannot. These qualities need to be essential components of your stepfamily.

Focus on What Works in the Stepfamily

Generally, there are certain factors that determine, overall, if your stepfamily is a success. But first, identify the specific traits in your own stepfamily that are meaningful to you.

Take a minute to write down what you consider important in a stepfamily, any stepfamily. This list can include things that you've always thought were important in a family that can also apply to the stepfamily; for example, tolerating one another's differences or being able to live with each other on a day-to-day basis. Try to list about five things that you feel would be critical to the success of a stepfamily.

Now let's do an exercise in how to measure the success in your stepfamily. Put your first list aside, and compile a second list. This second list is important because it will relate directly to your own stepfamily. Make another list, of five things or so, that you feel are *currently* success indicators in your stepfamily. This list would include things that you feel really work in your stepfamily. What does your stepfamily do right? What works with all the members of your stepfamily? What feels good about your stepfamily? Where do you feel the least problems exist in your stepfamily? What positives do people observe about you and your stepfamily? After thinking through these questions and any others that come to mind, jot down the five successes in your stepfamily. If you can list more, terrific. If you are having difficulty listing five, then you have work to do.

With your own list in hand, let's compare that to a general list and see how you and your stepfamily compare. Because each stepfamily is so individual in nature, however, different behaviors may operate within your own stepfamily. The list below can give you some overall guidelines to follow.

- Do you have good communication?
- Is there a sense of cohesiveness?
- Do each of you think of the stepfamily as your own family?
- Is everyone happy with the family?
- Do you encounter little or no conflict?
- Do members of your stepfamily see their future together?
- Is there minimal jealousy or anger?
- Do you look forward to spending time together?
- Is there a genuine love between the stepfamily members?
- Is there peace?

How did you answer these questions with regard to your own stepfamily? Do any or all of these ten items exist in your stepfamily? Clearly, if all ten are present to some degree in your stepfamily, you have or are on your way to a very successful stepfamily experience. If even some of them reflect your stepfamily, you are off to a good start. And if none of these ten appear within your stepfamily, then you have serious work ahead.

THE BENEFITS OF KNOWING YOUR STRENGTHS
AND WEAKNESSES

What are the benefits of knowing what works in your stepfamily? For one thing, it will help you know what you need to focus on, what to change, and what to leave alone. Writing down what runs smoothly in your stepfamily also gives each of you a chance to see that your stepfamily really does do some things right, because, so often in a stepfamily, everything can seem wrong. Seeing a list of positives encourages you and your stepfamily that you do have the ability to make this thing work! It can also be extremely helpful for bonding with your stepchildren. They should also review the list, contribute to it, and see the bigger picture of the stepfamily.

It's easy to get stuck in the day-to-day rut, and if little things don't go well, it sometimes feels as if the entire concept isn't working. Breaking down your family's successes in individual terms can be an eye-opening experience. It reduces frustration and allows each member of the stepfamily to feel good about what they have contributed to the success of the whole.

This exercise is also beneficial in identifying the positives in the bonding between the stepparent and stepchild. You and your stepchild can create lists of what you each admire in the relationship, and then compare notes. This exercise will help you to recognize if your stepchild envisions your relationship even remotely close to how you see it. It enables you to look into your stepchild's mind and see where he is at with this relationship, particularly if your stepchild isn't vocal about his feelings. It will also help your stepchild to see your perspective of things and what is important to you in bonding with him.

Defining Roles in Your Stepfamily

Whenever there is a discussion of stepfamilies, it can't be complete without talking about roles. But why are roles so important in a stepfamily? Think of it this way. At work, you have a role to play, a position that you hold, and the duties are defined for you so that you know what to do. If there were no roles at work, everyone would be running around doing a little bit of everyone else's job, and you would have instant and constant chaos. It's similar in a stepfamily. Each person has a role and different duties ascribed to that role. If everyone had the same role and responsibilities, how would you determine who the adults and the stepchildren would be? Who would be the authority figure? Who, in essence, would make the rules? If you did not know these answers, there would be chaos in your stepfamily. And that may be exactly how some stepfamilies operate.

But if you choose not to live in chaos, then there are certain things that you need to do, for example, defining roles. And if you define these roles early in the stepfamily, you may not have to live in chaos at all—ever!

Carrie and Trent have been married for five years. Trent has two children and Carrie has four children, bringing the family together to a healthy six children. The parents are both parent and stepparent; the children are both child and stepchild. Carrie and Trent had experienced a problem with the roles that each of them was supposed to play, and what roles the children were to play and at what time.

One of the issues in Carrie and Trent's stepfamily was that each of their own parenting styles was different, which meant that there were two distinct groups of kids in their family, raised by different parenting styles, and as a result, each responded to different roles and role models. It was confusing for Carrie and Trent, and they found it equally or more confusing for the children. Actually, their home had become quite chaotic, and they were not sure what to do about it.

First of all, we made a list of everyone in the stepfamily living in the house, categorizing them as either adult or child. Under these categories, Carrie and Trent drew up a list of responsibilities for each. Under adult, for example, they listed making the rules, making sure the rules are followed, mediating during conflicts, and other responsibilities they felt belonged to them as the adults. Under children, they comprised another list with input from the children. This list included obeying the rules, doing the chores without moaning and groaning, and various other responsibilities that the children had in the home. One of the major issues was who plays what role in terms of respect for one another. For example, under adult, Carrie and Trent were both listed as parent and stepparent. These rules often conflict and can be confusing to everybody. Trent and Carrie felt that they did not want to be seen as parent *or* stepparent but as parent only. Part of the chaos stemmed from the fact that their own children had no problem with the parent part, but their stepchildren—each others' children—saw the other adult as a stepparent, and it's difficult for stepchildren to get past that and think of their stepparent as a parent.

It's not always possible to be just a parent in a stepfamily. After much discussion between themselves and the children, Carrie and Trent reached the conclusion that, in their own stepfamily, it may not be realistic for both of them to be seen as parent and that each would also need to retain the title of stepparent. The children *saw* them each as parent and stepparent, and that is how the children identified them and responded to them. No matter how hard a parent or stepparent tries, the children may still see you in the role you play coming into the stepfamily. So, to reduce the confusion, understand this role. You may be a parent and stepparent; you may be a stepparent only; you may be a parent only. The same situation exists with the children; they may be a child and a stepchild, and in each role, they feel differently, react differently, and respond differently—just like you do. And that's okay.

WHY ROLES ARE IMPORTANT FOR THE STEPCHILDREN

How will knowing your roles strengthen the bond with your stepchild? Stepchildren want to know who you are and what role you will play in their lives. Are you their stepparent, are you the second parent, are you trying to be a friend—what? If they are continually confused about this, stepchildren may tend to withdraw from you. But if you are clear about your role as the stepparent, in whatever style you choose, your stepchildren will feel like their stepfamily is more functional than dysfunctional.

And stepchildren feel security in a functional family unit, just as in a traditional family.

Stepchildren also experience increased self-esteem if they are included in decision-making and role-setting. If your stepchildren are clear about who you are, and you are consistent with this, they will see you as a key player in the stepfamily. If you vacillate back and forth from stepparent to parent to friend, the stepchildren may have a tendency not to take you seriously and not feel good about accepting you as a strong member of the stepfamily. Stepchildren need consistency in the stepparent's responses to them. They need to know what to count on with you, and they need to feel assured of how you are going to react when they approach you. It is sometimes difficult for stepparents to grasp the significance of being consistent with the stepchildren, especially stepparents who do not have children of their own. Parents are familiar with how important this task is, and if, as a stepparent, you are experiencing a problem with being consistent, and your stepchildren are withdrawing from you, please discuss this with your partner to educate yourself about your partner's feelings and what would be the best way to proceed.

WHEN YOUR STEPPARENT ROLE CHANGES

Interestingly, the roles can also change, but your status as stepparent will not. For example, the relationship that you have with your stepchildren will evolve, just as relationships between parents and their children change as the children get older. You will relate to your stepchildren differently when they are five years old as opposed to when they are nineteen years old (at least we hope so!). How do you deal with a change in the relationship with your stepchildren? Simple. You adjust.

Your stepchildren will need different things from you at different stages of their lives, and it is up to you to be prepared to give them what they need and to be there for them. Depending upon the type of bond that you create with your stepchildren early in your relationship, the degree to which they need you will vary. As a stepparent, it is important that you be able to adjust to the needs of your stepchildren. Sometimes parents will say that they still see their children, into adulthood, as being seven or eight years old. Well, guess what: Generally, children don't appreciate that, so your stepchildren will be grateful if you acknowledge their maturity and growth into adulthood and independence. And there are many benefits for you and your spouse when they reach that stage—like privacy! And enjoying a relationship with your stepchildren as adults brings an entirely new meaning to your life as they begin to experience all of the pleasurable, and not so pleasurable, parts of life itself. Your stepchildren will struggle with careers, relationships, and many of the things that you have experienced. This is an opportunity for you to be a mentor and advisor to your stepchildren if, in fact, they can see you that way. Offering your stepchildren your expertise—when they ask for it—is a phenomenal way of maintaining your bond with them into adulthood.

What if This Isn't Working Out?

So, after doing everything you can to adjust to being in a family that wasn't your idea, you still feel that this simply isn't going to work for you. What happens now? The first and most obvious thing to do is to tell your partner. But do you share this kind of difficulty with your partner? This is certainly a sensitive issue, and you should take the time to examine and pinpoint exactly why you feel this way. Sometimes people don't like something for an unknown reason, and instead of trying to figure out why, it's easier to simply not like something. You need to be completely honest about what you are experiencing and why you feel the way you do. I can't stress enough how important it is to be open about this feeling *before* you become a stepfamily, but that isn't always possible. Sometimes stepparents don't begin to see the reality of a stepfamily until they are right in the middle of it. If that happens to you, there are several things that you can do.

Find a role in the stepfamily that does work for you. If it is not one of the roles or styles discussed in this book, then create a role for yourself that will fit your situation. Talk with your partner; what can you live with? What can your partner live with in this compromise? This will be one of the most difficult situations you will face as a stepparent, so you need to be open and honest, and to trust your feelings.

Talk to someone you trust. If that's your partner, great. If you feel you need to talk with other stepparents, even better. They will understand your dilemma and try to help you through it.

Better yet—start your own stepparenting group. This doesn't have to be a big deal—just a few stepparents getting together once a week, over coffee, to discuss issues that came up during that week and offer support and encouragement to the other group members. Remember that you are probably not the first stepparent in the world who feels as if he doesn't belong or fit into his stepfamily, but most of the time this can be resolved with the right amount of diligence, genuine caring, and love— and most of all, understanding.

Family therapy is available for stepparents and stepfamilies, and there are some excellent therapists who work with stepfamilies to help keep them together. If therapy may be an option for you, I would strongly recommend it for the sake of your stepfamily.

Even though this stepfamily may have not been your idea, the rewards of incorporating it into your lifestyle are tremendous. And once you have accepted the stepfamily into your life, it is time to focus on the unique connections between you and your stepchild.

6

STEP SIX

How to Begin Bonding with Your Stepchild

"When I met my stepchildren, it was important to me that we connect immediately. I didn't quite know how to do this since each was so different and unique. I knew one thing—that I would have to develop a relationship with each one in a different way; perhaps through hobbies or special interests. But where to begin?"

It can be overwhelming when you first meet the children of the person you love. The children are the people you most want to like you. Your new partner already likes you, but it's the children from whom you will seek the most approval. Why is that? As stepparents, we are aware that it's the relationship with the children that we will need to consciously work on most or all of the time. Our relationship with our partner comes more easily; it more closely resembles unconditional love. As we have learned in the book so far, the relationship with the stepchildren is not based on unconditional love and requires a conscious effort. This relationship, then, will require more energy.

Develop Your Own Relationship with Your Stepchildren

At first, many stepparents feel that the relationship with the children will grow out of the relationship with their spouse, like a plant. Picture your relationship with your spouse as the stem and the relationship with your stepchildren as the sprout off of that stem. In reality, what often occurs is that the stem consists of only the parent, and the stepparent branch is off by itself somewhere, dangling. As a result, the stepparent is mistaken in thinking that he will become close to his stepchildren through the relationship the children have with their own parent. The stepparent is often left out of things, feeling disappointment and, frankly, wondering why he entered into this stepfamily situation in the first place.

There are ways of preventing this disappointment, but more important, there are methods to help ensure that the stepparent is not left out. For instance, develop a relationship with your stepchild independent of her parents. If your stepchild visualizes you as an extension or an offshoot of her parent, then she will feel that you always agree with her parent. In a perfect world, you *might* agree with everything that your spouse says and does. Right now many of you are probably chuckling or howling with laughter at that thought! But as we know of the stepfamily, it is *not* a perfect world, and the stepparent is an individual with his own thoughts, feelings, goals, and opinions that he has a right to share. If you do agree with your spouse much of the time, great. However, if there are issues on which you disagree, it is important that your stepchildren know your feelings and respect how you feel.

As an example, let's look at shared visits. If your stepchildren visit every other weekend, they may be transported to your home by their other parent. Your stepchildren may feel that their parent should be able to stay at your house and visit, and this may be okay with your spouse, but it may be uncomfortable for you. You must be able to express your concerns about this situation, in a diplomatic and politically savvy way (because you will achieve more positive results) to your stepchildren so that surprises do not occur for you. It is imperative that your stepchildren not only hear your concern but understand why it exists, in order for them to see the difficulty that you are having. Why? Because if the stepchildren do not understand why you feel uncomfortable, they may begin to feel that you are simply being difficult, rude, or, often in their words, mean for not allowing their other parent to visit.

Children in stepfamilies must learn to understand the complexities of relationships much earlier than most children. This should not be perceived as a negative thing. It is a growth initiative for them and a leap into the world of juggling relationships at an earlier age, allowing them more practice for their adult lives. Children raised in stepfamilies are often much better equipped to handle relationships at work, with the many different opinions and issues to consider. And why not—they've been living it probably a good share of their lives right in their own family.

Why Your Stepchildren Must See You as an Individual

Often it is easier for stepchildren to see you as only their mom or dad's partner. Why? So that they don't have to work at a relationship with you. That sounds harsh but it's true. Stepchildren are kids—they want their lives to be hassle free, especially where their family situation is concerned. Their lives have been shaken up by the divorce and now a new parent enters the picture. Their first inclination will be to ignore you, in hopes that you will simply go away. Sound familiar? As adults, we may share these same feelings at work or in other interactions in our lives that we find challenging or unpleasant. So it's not unusual for stepchildren to feel this same way.

The problems that arise if your stepchildren see you as merely their parent's partner can occur gradually or quickly. It all depends upon your feelings. If it is important to you that your opinion be recognized, then the problem may surface quickly. If your stepchildren see you only as their dad's partner, then you will not be considered when decisions are made in the stepfamily, as far as the stepchildren are concerned. For example, let's say your stepchildren want to have friends over for pizza after school one day, and they ask their parent if that's okay. The parent says sure, because divorced parents may feel guilty and make quick, guilt-related decisions. The parent wants his children to be happy and will allow them to do many activities without checking first with you. Knowing this, the stepchildren do not ask you if it's okay, and normally, that may not be a problem. However, on this particular day, you have your book-reading club, also at your house. Guess what—they all show up. You flip. The stepchildren think they are in the right because their dad said it was okay. And there you are, feeling left out. Embarrassed. Angry. Resentful. This is only one incident. Now magnify these feelings, adding a little momentum each time an incident like this occurs. And what do you do? You may take it out on your spouse, which contributes to your spouse's concern that you can't handle this stepfamily situation. This is a good example of how small incidents can create serious misunderstanding, resentment, and failure.

The stepchildren must get to know you as the individual that you are. If they did, you would all be having the discussion about coordinating pizza parties and book clubs. If the stepchildren knew you individually, they would feel more comfortable with you and want to consider your schedule, too. The stepchildren would know that they need your permission as well as their parent's and that you are not merely an inanimate object in the home. Another benefit to having the stepchildren get to know you individually is that your spouse, their parent, will not want to interfere with your daily routines with the stepchildren. Why? Because the parent wants life to be simpler, too. The parent does not want to create conflict in the stepfamily; he is probably the one person in the stepfamily who wants peace more than anyone else. He will want you to discuss issues with his children about events in the home that affect the daily routine. He will not want to make decisions about everything; he will probably want you to handle some situations and will expect you to interact with his children in a certain way.

The stepchildren will need to form an opinion about you. This will occur naturally because you now live together. Of course, you will have the opportunity to form an opinion about your stepchildren as well. Sometimes stepparents start off on the wrong foot with their stepchildren, coming on too strong and telling them what to do, causing resentment. I encourage you to consciously think about the opinion that your stepchildren are forming about you.

Take a moment and review your experiences with your stepchildren. Have they been pleasant? Have these moments been stressed? If you feel that your interactions with your stepchildren have been difficult or unsatisfactory, now is the time to correct that. How? You can discuss your concerns with your stepchildren as a way of beginning a lifelong avenue of communication. Another effective strategy is to change your approach with your stepchildren. Once your stepchildren see that you are different, in a positive and comfortable way, they will respond better to you. This will also teach your stepchildren effective social skills that they can use outside of the stepfamily in school and work situations. As a stepparent, you can be instrumental in your stepchildren's development and growth. The key is to *develop* a healthy relationship with them.

How to Develop a Unique Relationship with Your Stepchild

An effective method for developing an individual relationship with your stepchild is through sharing a unique interest with her, particularly something you feel passionate about. This provides two things. One, by sharing your passion with your stepchild and encouraging her participation, you will share something special between the two of you. Your spouse may share in this, also, but it should be your passion and you should initiate it with your stepchild. Your stepchild will then see this as a unique bond between just the two of you. The second benefit of sharing your passion with your stepchild is that you have the opportunity to teach her about something in life that she can carry with her into adulthood.

Let's say your passion is sailing. You could take a short sailing adventure, maybe an afternoon, with your stepchild and expose her to what you know about sailing and why you enjoy it. Your stepchild will then see you in a different environment and not only in an authority position in the home. Your stepchild can begin to respect you for what you know and are willing to teach her. (And she may think it's cool and tell all of her friends how great you are, or at least take what you taught her and show off a little to her friends!) You are creating a memory with your stepchild, something that you can share exclusively, making your relationship solid and ongoing. Building memories builds long-term relationships.

Another idea might be to start an annual event with just you and your stepchild. For example, this could be a shopping trip to the Mall of America or a favorite place in your area. Or it could be a fishing getaway day or weekend with your stepchild. Take a minute now and think about things that you really enjoy. Make a list of the activities that come to mind such as playing chess, waterskiing, going to the coffeehouse, or gourmet cooking. You may also consider a holiday activity that could be unique just to you and your stepchild. For example, you may have a creative skill for carving pumpkins at Halloween that you can teach your stepchild.

One word of caution: Whatever the activity, be careful to consider that it is not the same activity that your stepchild already does with one or both of her parents, particularly the parent who does not live with you. This can cause hard feelings and may be viewed as you trying to compete with the other parent for the child's attention. That would not be a positive experience, and the idea of this exercise is to add to the stepchild's world of interests, not to antagonize the ex-spouse. One way to research this would be to discuss it with your spouse, who would probably know what activities his child enjoys doing with her other parent.

Review the list that you have just created and prioritize what would be doable, considering finances and time constraints. You will need to consider the age of your stepchild and, of course, get permission from her parents if it is an activity that requires travel or something the parents aren't familiar with.

Try doing the activity with your stepchild, and observe her feelings about it. You may need to experiment with different activities until your stepchild shows interest in one and wants to continue doing it with you. The idea is to create a scheduled activity with your stepchild that is an annual event to enjoy together. You can both look forward to it and plan for it each year, and you can revisit the pictures and always have a common topic to discuss with your stepfamily or the extended family.

You may think that participating in activities with your spouse and your stepchild may be enough to cement the relationship with your stepchild. You may wonder if you should include your spouse in on the annual event with your stepchild. The activities you engage in with your spouse and stepchild should be considered additional to the time when you bond alone with your stepchild. If you include your spouse all the time, your stepchild may see these excursions as events that she does with her parent, not with her stepparent, and you run the risk of being overshadowed. Just as your spouse needs time with his child, you also need time with your stepchild. In addition to that, as the stepparent, you need to represent something special in your stepchild's memory, too.

Don't Assume that You Will Grow Closer to Your Stepchild Through Your Partner

So you think, Why do I have to do all of the work in this relationship with my stepchild? It may be time-consuming, but think of it as a co-commitment that you made with your marriage to your spouse. You are willing to put time and energy into your marriage, and with marriage in a stepfamily, that also means a commitment to the child. Engaging in a romantic relationship with your spouse does not automatically make you a close part of the parent's relationship with her own children. It is unrealistic to assume that you will be instantly included in the closeness already established between the parent and the child. Why? Because that bond has existed since birth. The bond between a parent and child can be different, even within their own family, with multiple children.

Actually, the bond between parents and their child can be completely different, so it is unrealistic to think that even your spouse's ex-partner is an extension of the bond she has with her child. This becomes most evident in a divorce situation. When parents divorce, each parent works to secure a bond with the child, either out of guilt about the divorce and having to move out and live separately, or to compete with the parent who has custody. Whatever the reason, separate, divorced parents work hard to be sure the bond with their children remains intact. Unconditional love exists and survives the divorce; however, the insecurity of divorce can be powerful at times. So, even the parents may feel that they need to work at bonding with their children.

I would caution you to tread slowly, at first, when suggesting activities to your stepchild. He may be resistant and that is certainly understandable. Again, he may feel that you are only his parent's spouse, and that's it. You may burn out in pushing too hard with your stepchild, and worse, that could turn your stepchild off to you, as well. Rejection can be tough; no doubt about it. Take it slow. You can first suggest to your stepchild that you have a particular passion or interest, and let him take the initiative from there. If he expresses some interest or excitement about it, great. If not, give it time. Mention it again at some point when you and your stepchild are alone together, when you have his full attention. You can also ask your stepchild if there is something he is interested in—by chance, you may be an expert at it, or the two of you may have the same interest and can learn, research, and explore together.

HOW TO HANDLE REJECTION FROM YOUR STEPCHILD

If you do find that you are trying too hard and feeling disappointed, don't let yourself get burned out. This can put a tremendous strain on the romantic relationship with your spouse because all of the stepfamily relationships are interconnected. As you grow more disappointed about the perceived failure of your relationship with your stepchild, you become more resentful of the close relationship that your spouse has with her child. As a result, you may begin to feel like an outsider, not a part of their relationship. At the same time that you feel that your efforts are failing, your spouse is also working at the bond with her child—only that one is working. This can become extremely frustrating for the stepparent.

To watch while your stepchild consistently responds to his parent but rejects you is difficult. Even though mentally and rationally you know that this is a parent-child relationship, and that it is normal and healthy, it is still emotionally hurtful to you. Often stepparents will begin to resent their spouse for their own feelings of inadequacy with the stepchild. This is what you want to avoid. Why? Because it will strain the relationship with your spouse. Feeling resentful toward your spouse can mark the beginning of problems with romance and intimacy and, unfortunately, can lead to eventual separation. And if you continue to resent your spouse, think about the resentment that may be directed toward your stepchild. Relationships intertwined with resentment can be extremely difficult to manage. This can cause the breakup of your stepfamily, if you let it.

Jadie and Leonard had been married six months when tension began seeping into the household. Jadie had two boys from a previous marriage, and Leonard had two girls. The girls were fourteen and sixteen and the boys were younger, four and eight. Jadie was excited about the marriage and stepfamily idea. She had always wanted girls in addition to Judd and Slade, but she and her ex-husband had decided not to have any more children.

Soon after the marriage, Jadie showered Elise and Sammie, Leonard's children, with attention. She started buying them little gifts, constantly wanted to do their hair, and pushed "girl talks." At first, Elise and Sammie enjoyed the attention, but it didn't take long before they started to withdraw from Jadie. Jadie was confused by this, and, at the same time, the girls seemed to have more conversations with their father in private. Jadie, experiencing human emotions, began to feel uncomfortable about what she saw happening. As we explored her feelings more deeply, it became clear that Jadie was experiencing jealousy—

of her own husband! Jadie felt embarrassed, when, in fact, this is quite common in stepfamilies. Both parent and stepparent want a special relationship with the children. Leonard's children felt smothered by Jadie and didn't know how to tell her, so they turned to Leonard, asking him to convey how they felt to Jadie. Leonard, feeling badly about his children's dilemma, did just that. He approached Jadie and told her what the children were feeling. Jadie became upset, with the stepchildren and with Leonard, feeling like an outsider because the children didn't come to her, and also resenting Leonard for not asking the children to speak directly to her

DON'T ALLOW YOUR SPOUSE TO ACT AS MEDIATOR

This is one of the most common mistakes that occurs in the stepfamily—the parent relaying information to the stepparent from the stepchildren. Each time this is done, the stepparent feels alienated, and rightly so. It is imperative that the stepchildren be taught to communicate their feelings to the stepparent directly. Since the issue involves the stepchildren and the stepparent, the problem solving must take place between them.

When this type of situation occurs, usually all members of the stepfamily are left confused, particularly the stepchildren. Why? Because until you came along, the routine was for the stepchildren to go to their parent if they had a problem, and the parent probably fixed it. The stepchildren expect the same pattern will occur with you now. What is the best way to deal with that? Have a family meeting. All members need to sit down, set the rules of honesty without hurtful criticism, and air problems with the sole intent of finding a workable solution to fit the needs of everyone involved as best you can.

BE CAREFUL WHEN JUDGING YOUR SPOUSE'S RELATIONSHIP WITH THE KIDS

Simultaneously, it is important that the stepparent respect the separate relationship that her spouse has with his children. When we live with other people, it is natural to observe them, noticing their positive and negative traits. Stepparents and spouses will gradually develop opinions about each other as well. Stepparents will also form judgements about the relationship that their spouse has with their children. Of course, as a stepparent, you want your spouse to have a positive and healthy relationship with his children, one to which you can contribute. Compliment your spouse on the relationship that he enjoys with his children. Your opinion is important to your spouse, and knowing that you, his life partner, feel good about the relationship he has with his kids will help to build a solid and healthy bond between you. It's difficult to be divorced with children, and a supportive stepparent makes a winning combination for the stepfamily.

But what happens if you feel that your spouse does not have a healthy relationship with his children? Difficult situation. First of all, define what you mean by healthy. If you have observed that your spouse is not able to discuss issues well with his children, there is much arguing and shouting, the stepchildren withdraw from their parent or feel distant from him, this may present an opportunity for your help. But you must be honest in your observations. Ask yourself why you feel this way about your spouse and the stepchildren. Is it coming from your own anger or resentment toward him, as a result of the difficulty you are experiencing in the relationship? Are you jealous of their relationship? These are tough questions, but it's important that you are not overreacting and forming inaccurate opinions of your stepfamily.

If these factors don't exist, then write down what you have observed about your spouse and stepchildren that leads you to believe their relationship needs work. Review this, study it, and be realistic, because you have come to a crossroads. You have a choice of keeping this information to yourself or sharing it with your spouse in an effort to help improve his relationship with his children and the stepfamily as a whole. As a stepparent, you don't want to offend your spouse by blurting out that he could be doing this or that to improve his relationship with his child. So, if you feel that you can offer helpful insight and observation, approach this gently with your spouse.

Lancy and Daniel were the ideal couple. They loved each other completely and their stepfamily had all of the right elements for happiness. Lancy had no children, and Daniel came into the marriage with two daughters budding into adolescence.

After Lancy and Daniel were married, Lancy became aware that when Daniel had a discussion with his daughters, Lucy and Jenna, the girls looked disappointed afterward. They weren't angry, but they appeared frustrated. Lancy did not comment on this with Daniel, thinking that the girls were young and simply didn't agree with their dad about things.

This continued for a few months, until Lancy, feeling closer and bonding with her stepchildren, realized that Lucy and Jenna were coming to her for advice after discussions with their dad. Of course, Lancy was thrilled because she felt that she was finally a big part of the stepfamily. After a while, though, Lancy started to feel she was alienating Daniel with these conversations. She realized that Daniel felt this, too.

Lancy was in a dilemma. She had developed this relationship with the girls, but the girls were beginning to complain about their dad, saying he was old-fashioned and didn't understand them. Lancy was ten years younger than Daniel, and understood her stepchildren's perspective. She was at a point where she needed to resolve this situation between her stepchildren and her spouse.

Lancy chose to discuss this with Daniel by first expressing how delighted she was that the stepchildren were beginning to bond with her. Daniel was pleased with this, too. The following is a brief dialogue between Lancy and Daniel.

Lancy: Daniel, honey, the kids and I have been talking lately and doing more things together.

Daniel: I noticed that, too. I'm glad that you and the kids are getting along.

Lancy: They really are great kids.

Daniel: Thanks.

Lancy: And they're quite perceptive.

Daniel: What do you mean?

Lancy: Well, they're growing up and there are lots of things in the world that are different than when we grew up.

Daniel: That's for sure, Lancy.

Lancy: When I was a teenager, everyone was wearing those bell-bottom jeans with the flowers all over them. Remember those?

Daniel: Yeah, all the kids were wearing them.

Lancy: Seems like the craze now is the little tank tops with pictures of the peace symbol on them. Jenna and Lucy would look cute in those.

Daniel: Lancy, I think those types of things are too revealing and I don't want the kids wearing them.

Lancy: I understand, hon. I don't think they should show too much of their bodies either, and I told them that.

What if they wore a button-down shirt over the tank? Something fashionable so they would wear it. That way, they could wear the tank, feel included, and still look appropriate like you and I both want.

Daniel: That's a good idea. I hadn't thought of that. Could you go shopping with Lucy and Jenna to help them pick that out?

Lancy: I'd love to.

Notice how Lancy began gently discussing what the children wanted, careful to let Daniel know that she supported him when talking with the children. This was important because Daniel did not want to be alienated from his children, and, further, Lancy did not want him to feel threatened by her newfound relationship with the children.

Another key point for Lancy was that this newfound relationship with the children wasn't based on negativity toward Daniel, a point that needed to be clarified between Lancy and Daniel. You can discuss your concerns with your spouse about his relationship with his children, as long as you consider the ground rules of boundaries; a positive, healthy approach; and sensitivity.

And best of all, the conversation ended on a positive note, with Lancy, the stepparent, being invited by her spouse to spend more time with her stepchildren.

Don't Live Your Relationship with Your Stepchild Through Your Spouse

Have you ever known anyone from a distance? It may be your in-laws, or a coworker's spouse. This is a person who you have seen but really don't know very well. And if you don't know her very well, she would not be the first person you would call if you had great news to share, nor someone you might call on a whim to have lunch with or spend time together. She would not be a close friend or an intimate part of your world.

Sometimes a stepparent will have a relationship like that with his stepchild. He recognizes his stepchild physically but may not take the time to develop a bond with his stepchild and get to know her as a person. I've met stepparents who have felt that this was fine, and that it didn't cause any problems within their stepfamily. However, as we began to talk, there were clearly problems in the home; the stepparents had not yet made the connection, however.

Certain problems can arise in your stepfamily if you have a relationship with your stepchild through your spouse. First, your spouse may represent you to your stepchild from her view of you. This is fine if your partner has an accurate picture of you, but that doesn't always happen. Why? Sometimes when we express ourselves to other people, we unintentionally say things that may be different from what we intended. Think of someone that you may know who seems to be negative much of the time. That person may not even realize that they are giving that impression. This comes from the way our families communicated when we were growing up, or it can be a symptom of stress or unhappiness that we may be feeling in our lives. When people receive information from us, we may be thinking one way and voicing a completely different impression.

Even people who seem to know you very well, like your spouse, may not know the real you. And, if this is the case, and you rely on your spouse to relay information about you to your stepchild, it may be inaccurate information. This is not to suggest that your spouse is intentionally giving her child the wrong opinion about you, but information can be confused in the transfer of it. So, if you choose not to bond with your child directly, you take the risk of your spouse explaining you a bit differently to your stepchild than you may like.

This can be compared to a work situation. Think about the chaos that would occur if you communicated with your supervisor through a coworker! All kinds of things could be misinterpreted and confused. Well, that's what can happen in the stepfamily, as well, if communication and impressions are expected to be conveyed through other people. How would anyone get to know the real you?

What Happens If a Connection Is Not Developing Between Stepparent and Stepchild?

We all want to develop a connection with our stepchild. It's one of the most exciting elements when joining a stepfamily! But sometimes, bonding simply does not occur. What happens then?

There are several possible consequences that may occur if a connection doesn't take place, including tension within the stepfamily, secretiveness between the other members of the stepfamily, and a sense of paranoia on the part of the stepparent as well as the other stepfamily members. These are painful consequences for all members of the stepfamily, not only the stepparent.

Let's first look at tension in the stepfamily. Tension can develop for many reasons, but it will certainly develop as the result of having no connection with your stepfamily. We all know what tension feels like—that strain between people when we are not sure what to say to one another or how the other person may react. This leads to withdrawal from each other and eventually the communication breaks down completely, to a point where there is no communication, which can destroy your stepfamily. This may also destroy you, making you feel that you have failed and that you will never be a good stepparent. And it may also destroy your relationship with your spouse. Without a connection to the members of your stepfamily, each time you walk into the house, your spouse or stepchild may feel tension. Think of how uncomfortable that could be. Take a minute and imagine how wonderful your stepfamily would be without any tension in the home. Picture the look on your spouse's face without tension in the stepfamily. Picture the look on your stepchild's face. Now picture the look on your face if there was no tension in your stepfamily. Your stepfamily can be your haven—all it takes is some hard work, loads of understanding, and miles of patience.

Another possible consequence of not connecting with your stepchild is secretiveness. Secretiveness can be a nasty experience, especially when it's interpreted as being hurtful. Secretiveness can be destructive in a stepfamily. Why? Primarily because secretiveness is interpreted as alienation. If you do not develop a connection with your stepchild, the stepchild and parent will continue to form their after-divorce and new-stepfamily bonds—with or without you. As you observe their bonding progressing, and your spouse perhaps spends more time with his child, you may begin to experience some alienation. Most stepparents feel separate when the other members of the household are working on their relationships. A stepparent may see her spouse and stepchild conversing more often in private; this may occur because of the tension created by the stepparent's perceived disinterest in building relationships with the other members, or it may take place because the spouse and stepchild are unaware that they should be including the stepparent. Conversely, a parent may feel the need to be more private with his child to avoid problems with the stepparents. This may be perceived as secretiveness by the stepparent.

If this is happening in your stepfamily, and it bothers you, I would strongly suggest that you put some investigative work into this. Often a stepchild will want to speak to his parent alone, and that is only natural. However, a stepchild might do this without realizing how harmful it can be to the stepfamily's structure. To be a true stepparent, your spouse and stepchild must understand that you *are* to be included in family discussions, and it is up to the parent to open up to that, accept it, and explain it to his child.

169

If the secretiveness is occurring because of a negative reaction on your part, then you must be honest with yourself, and change, so that your spouse and stepchild will want to include you in conversations that affect the stepfamily. Secretiveness can be hurtful and destructive, whether the secrets are between you and your spouse, your spouse and his child, or between you and your stepchild. Openness and honesty are crucial to healthy, productive, and stable relationships based on trust.

A third consequence that may develop as a result of not connecting with your stepchild is a sense of paranoia. If you have reached this point in your stepfamily, I urge you to seek help through the resources that are comfortable for you. Again, we all have a sense of what paranoia feels like; this is an emotion commonly felt in the workplace as a result of feeling insecure about a conversation or event. Stepparents may feel a tremendous sense of insecurity in a stepfamily at different times. Some stepparents feel insecure at the beginning, after a difficult incident, or at particularly vulnerable times. Feelings of paranoia can occur as a result of secretiveness, but they can also be self-created by perceiving that you may not be accepted in your stepfamily the way you want to be.

You may feel a sense of paranoia if your spouse and stepchild appear to exclude you from activities they are engaging in together. If you are feeling like this, discuss it with your spouse. You need to validate these feelings and confirm them before you act on them. You may find that your feelings are unrealistic and that your spouse and stepchild do not see it that way at all, nor are they aware of how their actions look to you. Every stepparent and every stepfamily is different, so it is important that you examine your unique situation and determine the specific problems and solutions that will lead to your stepfamily's success.

Clark and Carolyn were married after a lengthy engagement, and as it turned out, this was a positive move for their stepfamily because they waited until the problems were resolved before they said their "I do." However, the lengthy engagement caused a certain amount of tension for Carolyn and for Clark, because they were both anxious to be married. But there were problems that were preventing that from happening, and neither knew how to resolve them.

Carolyn did not have any children, and Clark had come to the relationship with two young boys, Bobby and Miles. The boys had a good relationship with their father after the divorce, and Carolyn thought little about her relationship with Miles and Bobby. She felt that boys should bond with their father. As a result, Carolyn felt that the relationship with the boys and their father was all that their stepfamily needed.

When Carolyn spent more time at Clark's on the weekend, it wasn't long before the boys would do things that Carolyn felt were somewhat annoying. They'd leave their dirty clothes lying around their rooms, and Carolyn assumed that they expected her to pick them up. The boys would leave soda glasses, potato chip bags, and other leftovers in the living room. Carolyn felt that Clark would talk with the boys about this because, since he knew her so well, he clearly knew that these things bothered her.

When Clark did not talk to the boys about it and these same things continued to happen, Carolyn became resentful of Clark because she felt he wasn't defending her. When Carolyn complained to Clark, she was overly critical about the boys and argued in a sarcastic tone of voice. This only proved to incite Clark's anger.

Clark was in a fog because, one, he didn't think Carolyn's concern was a big deal, and two, he didn't want to discipline his boys because they'd had such a great relationship since the divorce and he didn't want to wreck it. Meanwhile, the boys were enjoying themselves, oblivious to what was brewing in the stepfamily. At the same time, Carolyn was not developing a connection with the boys, and she felt uncomfortable about telling them how she felt.

If Carolyn had developed a connection with the boys, this situation could probably have been resolved easily. She may have felt comfortable enough to tell them directly how she felt. Instead, she felt that this was something Clark should do. After all, these were Clark's children. Tension was developing in the stepfamily, and the boys felt it. As a result, they started talking with their dad about what might be going on, specifically, why Carolyn was acting "crabby." Again, if the boys had a connection with Carolyn, they could have asked her this directly rather than having to go through their dad. When Clark mentioned it to Carolyn, she became upset and resentful of both Clark and the boys.

Clark didn't know how to handle this; if he continued defending the boys, then Carolyn would be upset with him. But he couldn't go back to the boys and tell them that they had a role in creating this tension, because he didn't want to infer to the boys that they could be held responsible for some of the tension in the house. But the more Carolyn complained, the more angry Clark became at Carolyn. Each day, Clark and Carolyn's relationship was affected by this. At this point, the family needed a mediator to help resolve the issue and clarify roles in the pending stepfamily.

This is a good example of how little problems can build into major situations in a stepfamily and that how you present things to your spouse can determine how well issues can be resolved. It is also an example of how a stepchild can easily be confused by events that occur in the stepfamily if roles haven't been discussed and clarified prior to living together. The stepchild does have a responsibility in helping to build a connection with the stepparent. This will contribute greatly to the success of the stepfamily.

You may be experiencing this type of situation in your stepfamily right now. If so, I would encourage you to examine several things. One, is your concern about your stepchild's actions valid and realistic? Do you have a connection with your stepchild where you can discuss it with her directly? Is it something that you should tell your spouse about? Can you explain it in terms that will not upset your spouse? Above all, it is important to remember that your stepchild is your spouse's child and you must be sensitive when sharing information with your spouse.

If you do experience some difficulty connecting with your stepchild, be patient. Developing an emotional bond does take time, but there are other means of growing closer to your spouse's children. Find what will work for you.

7

Realize that Love Comes Later

"Her kids act like they don't even like me. I can't understand it. I showered them with gifts—and nothing. I expected them to love me right away."

Love. Is there any other feeling in the world that makes us uncomfortable if we don't receive it back immediately from someone? No, there isn't. There is something annoying about perceiving that someone who we want to be close to does not love us. It's not only frustrating, it's downright threatening. If we extend love to others, we expect it in return. Immediately, we think, Why don't they feel the same way about me as I do about them? And then, What's wrong with me? When this set of insecurities starts up, it's one point for insecurity and none for us.

It's basic human nature, right? We give love; we receive love. For the majority of relationships, this is true. But we are talking about a stepparent-stepchild relationship—a whole other ball game, my friends. You know those rules you have always followed about expectations and gut feelings? Well, throw them out because this is a new game, and you are now in unfamiliar territory.

The Meaning of Love in a Step Relationship

What does love mean anyway? Specifically, what does love mean in a step relationship? First, define what love means to you in a relationship that you currently have. In the relationship with your spouse, love means intimacy and a longing to be together. If you have children, love equals a lifetime of caring, support, and responsibility. In the relationship with your parents, love is the answer to their supporting, bearing, and raising you. If you have a friend who you love, you can depend upon that person to be there when you need to talk, or eat cheesecake, or take a walk. It all makes perfect sense, right?

In a step relationship, love can exist but it also often doesn't make sense, at least initially. It can mean something quite different from what you normally perceive as love. Why? Because you are feeling love toward someone who was introduced to your life through a relationship based on love with someone else— your spouse. There is no question that you love your spouse. But, in the beginning as a stepfamily, you wonder whether you love your stepchildren. Every stepparent asks himself or herself this question, either silently or aloud to their spouse. It's a natural question in a stepfamily situation, so don't feel guilty about it. Now ask yourself while reading this, Do you love your step-children?

If you said, yes, great, you are off to a good start in your stepfamily. If you are hesitant about this answer, don't feel bad. You are not alone. Many stepparents question whether they love their stepchildren. Many stepparents don't even know what it means to love their stepchildren.

Stepparents often mistake loving their spouses as also loving their stepchildren. It's as if some magic wand was waved over you, when you married a parent, that covered the love for your spouse *and* the children automatically. It doesn't generally work that way. It takes work to love someone else's children. That is one thing you can rely on in a stepfamily. The problem arises when you, as a stepparent, feel pressure to love your stepchildren immediately. Sometimes it's pressure from your spouse. Sometimes it's pressure from the extended family—on both sides. And sometimes it is simply self-created pressure, that if you don't love your stepchildren, then there is something wrong with you. And you feel if you admit that to anyone on planet Earth, then you truly are the wicked stepparent.

Human beings repeat negative statements to themselves on a daily basis. Stepparents may do this even more often! You continually berate yourself for not meeting the expectation of your role in the stepfamily. One of these expectations is that you love your stepchildren. Think about this: *You love your stepchildren.* It is a huge task for humans to love one another. There is risk. There is fear of rejection. There is the uneasiness of feeling that you are giving love but not receiving it in return. With all of these thoughts occurring simultaneously, it's a wonder there is any energy left for the emotion itself—love!

In a stepfamily, love can mean one thing—or many things. Love can mean a love-you-no-matter-what feeling. If you feel that type of love for your stepchild, that's great. But you may not love your stepchild unconditionally, now or ever. But there are other ways to feel the same way that love makes us feel, and that's what we need to explore in step relationships.

ACCEPTANCE AS A FORM OF LOVE

The one word that best describes love in the step relationship is acceptance. Now let's deconstruct the word acceptance. What does it mean to accept someone? It means to understand, tolerate, and not judge another person. Acceptance can also mean that you like another person and support him in his goals. But it is different than love. How? Acceptance still offers us a degree of control. To say we accept someone allows us to have boundaries from that other person. What does this mean? Well, think of someone that you love—your spouse, your parents, or your siblings. In love, particularly unconditional love, you freely and willingly share your thoughts, your feelings, and your life, basically without giving it much thought. When we accept another person into our lives, we do it at our speed or when we are ready. We can do it more slowly if we need to, or we can do it rapidly. But we have the ability to make that decision when it comes to acceptance or tolerance. Can it still feel good? You bet. It may even feel better because you are making the decisions about it.

Take a minute and think about what acceptance means to you. Now apply that meaning to your stepchild. Can you accept your stepchild at this level? This is a hard question to ask yourself, but you must. Accepting your stepchild on the level that is comfortable for you is key in your step relationship. And rather than forcing the idea of love into this relationship, break down the concept of love into acceptance to make it manageable in your relationship with your stepchild. You will save yourself the disappointment of not being able to feel love for your stepchild immediately. And, secondly, you avoid the shame of not meeting the societal expectations of being a stepparent because you feel you don't love your stepchild as completely as you are supposed to.

When you focus on accepting your stepchild, you can take the weight off of your shoulders of being the one who is expected to make this relationship loving. That isn't necessarily your job as a stepparent. Your job is to help make the stepfamily work, and accepting your stepchild one step at a time is the way to build a long-lasting relationship and supportive family structure. If you accept your stepchild in whatever capacity you can, you have created the opportunity for your stepchild to interact with you in return and begin to build a relationship. If love does build between the two of you as a result of your initial acceptance, then that love will be developed and nurtured by both of you. Ideally, love is a two-person journey. When you feel love, you feel good, and feeling good about other members of your stepfamily is a significant step toward stepfamily bonding.

Hal and Linda became engaged when they decided both were ready to start building their stepfamily. Hal had two teenage daughters, Jacy, fourteen, and Lara, twelve. When Linda first met the girls, she liked them but she did not feel a strong connection with them. She didn't tell Hal how she felt. She didn't think it was important because Linda felt that Hal and his ex-spouse would be involved with the girls, and that she would play a secondary role in their lives.

As soon as she and Hal started informing people that they were getting married, Linda was stunned when her friends said things such as, "Well, you must love those girls to want to marry someone with children" or "You know, you'll have to love his children in order to make this marriage work." Suddenly, getting married seemed not like a romantic idea, but like a monumental task—all Linda could think about was that she *had* to love Hal's kids or the marriage wouldn't work.

Linda hadn't given a great deal of thought to what her relationship with Jacy and Lara would be, but she certainly did after hearing comments like that. Suddenly, Linda felt incredible pressure to love the girls, but there was a problem. She didn't love them. As a result, Linda put herself through Guilt 101 and Wicked Stepparenting 102. She didn't feel comfortable discussing this with Hal and she didn't want to talk to anybody else for fear of being judged. Linda worried herself into a frenzy. And she almost called off the wedding because of it.

After we discussed the problem at length, Linda agreed to discuss this with Hal in the therapy session so that Hal would not become defensive or misunderstand this sensitive situation.

Once Hal understood that Linda truly liked the kids but didn't love them—yet—he was fine. Actually, Hal comforted Linda by revealing that he didn't expect her to love his children right away. He explained that if Linda gradually came to love Jacy and Lara, he would be quite happy. But also, if the kids and Linda did not ever love each other, but accepted and tolerated one another, Hal would be fine with that. This was a huge burden off Linda's shoulders, and a relief to know what Hal's expectations were *before* they said "I do."

Healthy Relationships Resolve Conflicts with Ease

Conflicts occur all the time, even with the people we love. Why? Because we are different people with different thoughts and behaviors. It's how we handle conflict that makes a difference in how our relationships affect us.

Think of a conflict you may have had with a coworker or someone who is not a member of your family, perhaps a neighbor. Think of how the conflict developed and how it was resolved—if it was resolved. Now think of how you felt. Most human beings do not like conflict. In fact, we try to avoid it if we can. Conflict is uncomfortable, but it occurs regularly in the workplace and in families, particularly stepfamilies. In the workplace, conflict resolution is slow and methodical, because generally the relationship between coworkers is not based on love. It is based on a variety of other factors such as respect or disrespect, and knowledge, but there is a known distance between coworkers. You work together, but you leave at night for separate personal lives. Under these circumstances, conflict may be more difficult to resolve.

In stepfamilies, there is also conflict. Every stepparent should take a course in conflict resolution. The step relationship can be compared to that of coworkers, with the issue of possibly lacking respect for one another. So, without respect, caring, a love connection, or similarities in personal lives, imagine how difficult conflict is to resolve. Without a basic caring for one another, which provides compassion and understanding, resolving any conflict is difficult at best. When people who love each other argue, there is a common ground between them that includes not only compassion and understanding but also a willingness to forgive. Disagreements resolve easier and more quickly between people who love one another, so it is to your advantage to love your stepfamily members, on some level, in order to keep conflicts to a minimum and reach resolutions more effectively.

Why We Expect Love in a Stepfamily

We expect love in a stepfamily because it is a form of family. Families are supposed to be about love, and loving one another equally, without reservations. Family members should care about each other and support one another, right?

In the stepfamily, the ideal situation would be if all members truly loved one another, unconditionally. For a large percentage of stepfamilies, this type of love doesn't exist—at least not initially. But love is expected to develop in the stepfamily just as in any other form of family. Do you know other stepfamilies that appear to get along well and never fight? You may think, Wow, they are special because they love each other and don't have a problem with it. Relax, this is common. Things aren't always as they appear, and nine chances out of ten, the stepfamily you are thinking about has either gone through significant conflict to get where they are, or they are careful not to let others see their difficulties.

Who expects people in stepfamilies to love each other? Everyone—your parents, his parents, your grandparents, his grandparents, the neighbors, your pastor. There is so much pressure to love each other that it can suffocate a stepparent who doesn't expect it. And if you don't feel the instant love that everyone else expects, it is common to feel guilt about not loving your stepchildren!

Your partner will expect either that you love his children or that you have some type of connection with them. In my experiences, the majority of parents secretly wish for their new spouse to love the children. But parents also know that it is unrealistic to assume that another person will love their children instantly, so they encourage you to work at it. This is a reasonable request. You should work at this. Why? Because you will also expect some type of connection with your stepchildren. They are a part of your new spouse, and therefore, they are now a part of you. Just how hard you work at that connection is up to you.

DISCUSS EXPECTATIONS WITH YOUR PARTNER
AHEAD OF TIME

You may want to discuss this with your spouse so that you have the same idea of what you are trying to accomplish with her children. Maybe your spouse doesn't expect you to love her children. Maybe she wants you to be friends with her children or share in the disciplinarian role. Whatever the expectation, I encourage you to define and develop it.

Kent and Sherri were making wedding plans which, of course, included the children. Sherri had two sons, Derek and Ethan, from a previous marriage. Their father was not a big part of their life, and Kent was a new male figure for them. Kent, however, did not have children and he did not plan on having children of his own. He was playing a new role that was foreign to him in this relationship.

Sherri assumed that Kent would be a father figure to Derek and Ethan, just as he would be a husband to her. Kent felt uncomfortable with the boys and, as a result, did not plan to spend much time with them—they were Sherri's kids, and his connection with them would be through Sherri. Sherri thought that this would change once they were married, but she didn't mention it. She didn't want Kent to think she was criticizing him, and she knew that marrying someone with two kids was not an easy task. After Kent and Sherri were married, however, Kent's relationship with the boys did not change. He did not take an active, fatherly role with them. This frustrated Sherri because Kent was not doing what she expected him to do. Sherri, however, would talk with Derek and Ethan about Kent being their father now, and how they needed to give him time to become the father they so much needed and wanted.

The situation did not change until one day Derek called Kent Dad. Kent was stunned because he didn't expect to have to be a father to Derek and Ethan. As Kent was sharing this incident with Sherri, it became clear to both of them that they didn't have the same expectations about the parental roles in their stepfamily. Kent was uncomfortable with the dad role because he simply didn't know how to be a dad, but he felt insecure about telling Sherri because he didn't want to disappoint her.

This is a classic example of what occurs in stepfamilies when people fail to discuss these details prior to the marriage. Stepfamilies will encounter unnecessary conflict and then find themselves in a tense and difficult situation, with escalating anger and few effective tools, such as compassion, love, and understanding.

The Stepchild's Responsibility in the Relationship

Stepchildren need to know that their parent expects a connection between their stepparent and them. Why? Because stepchildren will find a reason not to connect with you if they don't have to. Remember, they didn't choose you, their parent did, so their responsibility to you is limited. If stepchildren are given the message that you need to do all the work to please them, your stepfamily will have a problem. You will feel the pressure to make this work and the rejection if it doesn't. So, please, give the stepchildren responsibility in relationship-building. It will help them later on in life when they engage in their own adult relationships.

Your stepchildren will need a roadmap to follow when attempting to love an outsider. This is not an easy task and, as adults, we understand that. Stepchildren will need guidance and support while being encouraged to form a connection with their stepparent. This may be the first time that the stepchildren have been in this position, so keep this in mind if it doesn't go smoothly right away. The biological parent will have a role in teaching and guiding the stepchildren to developing a connection with the stepparent. Without the support of the parent, the stepchildren may not be able to accomplish this necessary step in the relationship with the stepparent.

First, the parent needs to explain to her children why she wants them to connect with you. The stepchildren may feel that they will connect with you through their parent. This may be fine if the stepchildren are adults, supporting themselves. However, if the stepchildren are living in the same household, it would be difficult not to have any connection between you. It would be like you are all floating around in the household, never speaking or touching or accidentally running into each other at the front door. That is, of course, unrealistic. Inevitably, at some point, you will connect, so why not do this with intent and planning to avoid conflict further down the road?

EXPLAINING YOUR VISION TO YOUR STEPCHILD

Once the stepchildren and their parent have discussed why it is important, the next step is to involve the stepparent. The stepchildren may feel just as pressured to love you, so this would be a good time to put them at ease about that. Lay out your plan of action. Let your stepchildren know how involved you want to be with them. Ask your stepchildren how comfortable they are with your plan. This will begin the process of your connection because your stepchildren will feel good that you *asked* them and didn't just tell them how it was going to be. It's especially important to ask your stepchildren rather than tell them because they probably weren't asked about their parents' divorce, so they don't feel in control of anything. That's a tough spot for kids to be in, so you'll need to give them a break on that one.

Talking with your stepchildren about how you envision your relationship will also encourage their input, allowing them a degree of control or empowerment in the stepfamily. Kids tend to act out when they feel out of control, so you may need to remind them that they have the opportunity for input at any time. Your relationship with your stepchildren will continue to grow and change, so you will experience conflict along the way. Try to look at it in a positive way, even though this is difficult, especially when you feel angry or disappointed. As the stepparent, you have the tools to work through conflict—your stepchildren may not have these tools. Therefore, you need to be the one to initiate resolution.

Why Love Cannot Be Forced

When we first become stepparents, we feel happy and positive. We've recently married and we're ready to start our new family life. It's only natural to think that your new stepchild will want you to be his new parent right away. After all, you have just accepted this role. Many people would like to feel that they have contributed to the nurturing and guidance of kids but there's one problem with this in a stepfamily. The stepchild is not your biological child. Therefore, your stepchild will not automatically want you to be his nurturer or guidance counselor. Becoming a stepparent means a great many things, but one thing it doesn't allow you is automatic unconditional love privileges. This is one of the greatest disappointments for new stepparents. It's not only a letdown, but stepparents soon discover that it takes more work to achieve a positive image in their stepchildren's eyes than they ever imagined.

As a stepparent, you must earn the love or acceptance of your stepchild. You're probably thinking, That's not fair, and you are right. It's not fair to you, but think of how the stepchild might view this. Why should he be expected to love you, unconditionally, immediately? He doesn't know you. As adults, we wouldn't expect someone we don't know very well to love us that way. We know that it takes time to build that trust and love. It isn't any different for a stepparent and a stepchild. You meet as strangers. You have one common denominator, your spouse, his parent. You must build a relationship, initially, based on this common denominator, and only later will you be able to build a separate and meaningful relationship once you've passed that first step. If I were asked, "What is the one key factor that will help ensure a healthy stepfamily relationship?" my answer would be quite simple—the parent. She is the answer to building the stepfamily, one step at a time. She is also the answer to why love cannot be forced.

It is imperative that you discuss this sensitive issue with your spouse first. Why? You may assume that your spouse wants you to love her children. That may not be the case. Parents look to their children for support just as the children look to their parents for it. Once parents divorce, they become vulnerable, out in the world alone again, only this time with children. They are looking for a partner in life, but now that partner needs to not only be compatible with them but to also be compatible with the children. Working with stepfamilies, it has become clear that parents, through their protectiveness and vulnerability, feel threatened by other adults moving ahead too rapidly in a relationship with their children. This is perfectly normal for many reasons. Parents don't want their children hurt if their relationships with new partners don't work out. They also don't want their children confused by the influence of new people and change. They are adjusting to a new life with their children and too much too fast may cause unnecessary disruption. It is to your advantage, as a stepparent, to be sure of how your mate feels about your relationship with her children. How far does she want you to go? Does she want you to eventually love them? Or is liking them or accepting them okay? These questions are not only reasonable to ask, but necessary. Why? Because the parent needs to be supportive to both you and her children as this relationship begins to develop.

EARNING YOUR STEPCHILD'S LOVE

So how do you earn the love of your stepchild? Simple—over time. You will need to get to know your stepchild slowly to understand how he feels about loving you. Your stepchild may have no intention of loving you, just putting up with you. This is a common feeling among stepchildren, even stepchildren who are adults. (I already have two parents. Why do I need another one?) So the key is to present yourself not simply as another parent but a benefit to his life. Choose what kind of stepparent you want to be, and intertwine that with his expectations to create a workable and satisfying relationship for both you and your stepchild. It's like being a new employee in a company. You need to present yourself to this organization as a benefit in order to gain respect, satisfying working relationships, and maybe even a raise for accepted performance. The "raise" that you receive in the stepfamily is a healthy and fulfilling relationship with your stepchild, once you have presented yourself as a benefit to the stepfamily.

YOUR STEPCHILD'S PARTICIPATION

Of course, you and the parent are not the only ones who have a responsibility in this new family. Why? Your stepchild also has a responsibility to you as the stepparent. She has certain boundaries, namely, that she cannot act like a complete monster toward you while you are continuing your efforts toward trying to bond with her. She must also try to reach out to you by including you in her extracurricular activities at school or making you feel like one of the family. The stepchild can offer the stepparent a degree of comfort in the stepfamily by initiating conversations with you, inviting you to participate in an activity with her, and not walking on eggshells around you if you happen to be alone together in the house. Sometimes a stepchild does not realize how her actions can affect her parent's and stepparent's feelings or reactions. A stepchild often feels that the adults will do what they want anyway, without considering the stepchild. This may appear true to the stepchild, but as a stepparent, you *are* aware of the child and what she may be thinking. This is another reason for stepparent guilt; we are always thinking that we should have said or done something differently because then our stepchildren would like us *faster*.

A FOUNDATION OF TRUST CAN LEAD TO LOVE

Build a foundation with your stepchildren based on trust and a genuine liking for each other. This could eventually lead to love, but you need not be so focused on loving each other right away. This takes the pressure off both the stepchild and the stepparent. The risk is that you may truly *not* like each other, but that is yours to assess individually and personally.

As stepparents, we pressure ourselves to want to love our stepchildren. What if we just liked them? There is nothing wrong with that. Besides, like can lead to love, so you are well on your way if you like your stepchildren. Is it okay to like your stepchildren without loving them? Yes, absolutely. Without feeling the need to love people who came to you by accident, you may develop a longterm friendship with your stepchildren, particularly when they become adults. Sometimes, however, this doesn't come easy, and it's understandable. We meet new people frequently; some we like, some we don't. As a stepparent, you are expected to like your stepchildren because they are your spouse's kids. But, again, there wasn't a choice involved with the stepchildren, only with the spouse. So, you may have stepchildren that you don't even like. It's okay to admit it. This does happen. I have found, however, that stepparents who feel they don't like their stepchildren experience this for a reason that they can control. Either their spouses are continually siding with the children or the stepparents are jealous of the stepchildren. These issues *can* be worked through, and the stepparents can eliminate these feelings of not liking their stepchildren and be free from the stress of feeling guilty about it.

WHEN LOVE IS IMPOSSIBLE

But what happens if the love simply does not develop? Don't worry, it's not the end of the world, though it may feel like it at times. Look at it this way, do you love your coworkers? Probably not. But you see them and work with them every workday. And how do you do that? You find mutual ground with them and you learn to tolerate one another. It is similar with a stepchild. You may never love your stepchildren and they may never love you. Give yourself a break. It doesn't mean that you have failed as a stepparent. If love does not develop with your stepchild, there is something you can do about it.

First, don't give up. You are not a failure. You are not a wicked stepparent. You are not incapable of loving someone else's child. It takes two, and the two personalities that are involved may simply not make a love connection. So, what do you do? You meet halfway, or as close to the middle as you can. You find mutual ground. You stop aiming for love as the only plateau that your relationship can reach, and you start slower and break it down into more manageable pieces. Examine what you and your stepchild do have in common. What same things do you like? What same beliefs do you have? What same foods do you like? Start with anything that you agree on and go from there. Human beings are cautious animals. We don't like to jump in with both feet without some security. So, with your stepchild, start small and proceed slowly.

Approach this situation with your stepchild as a project. Shoot for an achievable goal. Can you mutually respect each other? Respect is often easier than love, especially if your stepchild feels that you are an intruder or may have caused the breakup of his parents. It will also be interesting to see how your stepchild reacts if you explain to him that you don't *expect* him to love you. After his mouth drops to the floor, you may have just created the perfect climate for him *to* love you—a relaxed and nonpressured environment in which to nurture feelings of caring and love.

Strengthening the Bond with Your Stepchild

Whether your relationship with your stepchild develops into love or mutual respect, the basic groundwork has been laid for the success of your stepfamily. Once members of the stepfamily feel comfortable with their roles, boundaries, and relationship roadmaps, the stepfamily can begin to move ahead as a whole unit.

Once love or mutual respect has been established between you and your stepchild, you will begin to feel a comfort level in the home. This is primarily because the pressure to be close will be off. Neither of you will feel the need to avoid one another because the rules about your relationship will be more clear and better understood. Your spouse will also be relieved once the relationship direction is more clear, and there will be a renewed sense of caring between you. Your spouse will see you as a positive addition to the family, and fall in love with you all over again, knowing that you like, maybe even love, her children, and that you won't try to distance her from her children. This is an amazing moment in the life of your relationship together. Too many stepparents and their spouses don't stop to appreciate this moment. It is a landmark in your relationship, as well as in the stepfamily. This is the moment when you know, for certain, that your spouse approves of your relationship with her child. The moment may be marked by a glance and smile by your partner. Your spouse may tell you directly how happy you have made her. Or it may happen when your whole stepfamily is together.

One weekend, Mia and Charlie didn't have plans because

Charlie's kids were scheduled to visit. Charlie had two daughters, Lizbeth, fifteen, and Darcy, twelve. Charlie had to work for a short while in the morning, so he left early and returned home around noon. It was Saturday, and Mia was planning to do some cleaning around the house and maybe read a little.

Around noon, Charlie came home. Mia didn't hear him come in. As Charlie walked around the corner into the living room, he saw Mia and his daughter, Darcy, sitting on the floor playing chess. Mia looked up at Charlie and he had a look on his face, as Mia described it later, "of love, a deeper love." Mia said she hadn't seen Charlie ever look at her like that before.

As Charlie related the story, he indicated that at the moment when he turned the corner in the room and saw Mia laughing and playing this game with Darcy, he knew, at that moment, that he had made a wonderful choice in Mia as his lifetime partner. Mia and Charlie both said they will never forget that moment, and years later, when I saw them by chance on the street, they both related that same story to me. I could hear and feel the tenderness between them, at this, the start of their bonding stepfamily.

The benefit of strengthening the bond with your stepchild is tremendous for you, your partner, and your stepchild. It truly is the beginning of life for you as a stepfamily. You begin to look forward to building your healthy stepfamily—healthy because of all the moments you will share as a stepfamily including the good and the bad, when you will be there to support one another. For a stepparent, this is a life-affirming moment because maybe for the first time as a member of this stepfamily, you truly are looking forward to the future.

8

The Future with Your Stepchild and Your New Family

"I want to develop a good relationship with my stepchild, not only for now but for the future, too. There will be high school proms, graduations from college, weddings, and maybe even stepgrandchildren. I want to be a part of each event in my stepchild's life. But will my stepchild want me to be intimately involved in events in her life?"

All stepparents think about the future with their spouse, and, ultimately, with their stepfamily. An important part of that future vision involves what your future will look like with your stepchild. If you haven't given much serious thought to the future, I encourage you to do that now. Just as your spouse is dreaming of his son's high school graduation, his son's wedding, and his first grandchild, you, too, will need to dream these dreams about your stepchild. After all, you will be sharing in all of the adult firsts, along with your spouse and his ex-spouse.

But what role will you play? That question crosses every stepparent's mind once the relationship with her stepchild begins to form and evolve. But, you may think, isn't playing a role in my stepchild's future a given? Why is it important what role I will play in my stepchild's future as his stepparent?

Simple. It is one thing to develop a comfortable daily routine with your stepchild within your stepfamily and the comfortable surroundings of your home. It is quite another to maintain this comfort level when you are involved with other members of your stepchild's family who are not around you every day in your stepfamily's life. Within your stepfamily, you and your spouse are at center stage to your stepchild. Together you make the decisions and are the focus of your stepchild's world. Once events take place that include not only your extended family but your stepchild's extended family, the stepparent sometimes becomes so secondary that you may feel invisible. In these situations, your stepchild's world expands greatly to include his other parent and family, including grandparents, aunts and uncles, cousins, and perhaps additional stepfamilies included in that family network. You, as the stepparent, assume the backburner status, and this is sometimes a difficult adjustment, particularly given all of the energy you have invested in this special bond with your stepchild.

Lifetime Milestones for You and Your Stepchild

It is important that you develop a plan with your stepchild for future events in both of your lives. Plan ahead for these events with your stepchild because it will give her the clear message that you are here for the longterm, and that you plan to share in her achievements. It will help your stepchild realize how much you care about her and want to participate in her lifetime milestones, and that you want her in yours. When these milestones begin, this will be a wonderful momento for you and your stepchild to review and reminisce about. Remembering how you planned for these events together will be a special moment between the two of you.

Planning ahead eliminates the anticipated stress of worrying about what kind of role you will play in these stepfamily and extended-family activities. And, finally, you are creating a lifetime of memories with your stepchild. So, by planning ahead, you can build memories with your stepchild based on the special bond that you have worked so hard to create.

GRADUATIONS

As stepparent, you will attend your stepchild's graduation. Most high school graduation ceremonies ask the parents to stand up to be recognized for their child's achievements. Often the child then delivers a flower and hugs his parents. Both parents will be involved in this. The stepparent should be included, too. I have discussed this with stepparents who were excluded from this type of recognition, only to find it confusing for themselves and the stepchild. This is understandable. Imagine if you were suddenly in that situation with your stepchild without a prior clue about what might be taking place. The stepchild may not know what to do in this situation and unintentionally does not include you in the recognition. By planning ahead and determining your role, the pressure will be off both you and your stepchild. It's also a good idea to plan now to avoid any feelings of being left out or of simply feeling excluded. Planning ahead will also prevent any awkwardness in those special moments for your stepchild assuring him that he handled the situation in a socially appropriate manner.

College graduation can be handled in the same way. The stepparent should be recognized along with the parents. There may be other ways that the high school or college your stepchild attends recognizes parents specifically, so I encourage you to apply this information to your specific situation.

WEDDINGS

Weddings are wonderful, and if there is a wedding in our family, we all want to participate in it. There is the same feeling in a stepfamily. It is important for your stepchild to understand that you want to be included in her wedding. What do I mean by included? You should play an active role in the wedding activities. Just as the parents will hold the status of mother and father of the bride or groom, you should be recognized for your role in the stepchild's life. The various activities you participate in at the wedding will be determined by your stepchild, as it is her wedding, but you should plan ahead with your stepchild, offering suggestions that she might not have considered. Walking down the aisle may still be reserved for the parents, but discuss this with your stepchild—she may feel differently and want to include you. You should be in the receiving line after the ceremony, greeting the guests attending, and you should be seated in a reserved place at the meal, or you may want to offer a toast at the wedding. These are some suggestions to get you started in planning your role at your stepchild's wedding. You and your stepchild may have special ideas and you may want to consider researching this with a wedding consultant, tapping into a consultant's experience with step weddings.

STEPGRANDCHILDREN

You can have fun with this one! But, as with all of the other events in your stepchild's life, discuss your role in your stepgrandchild's life, such as sharing in the babysitting, and maybe even sharing in the birth! You may make a great birthing coach for your first stepgrandchild. You will also need to discuss your role in religious ceremonies that may take place, such as a baptism. Coordinate gift buying for the baby with the other parent, always taking the initiative in preventing hurt feelings with your stepchild's extended family members. You may be planning to start a small bank account for your stepgrandchildren, which should be discussed with your stepchild and your spouse.

Of specific importance would be a discussion about how often, and when, you'd like to see your stepgrandchild. Respect your stepchild's feelings if he wants you to call ahead or schedule this in advance. Remember, this may have been what you had requested when your stepchild was younger with visits from his other parent. It may be like coming full circle in your stepfamily, where you were the role model to your stepchild and taught him appropriate and respectful ways of dealing with situations in your stepfamily that would comfortably accommodate everyone involved. Now it may be his turn to want to request this.

RETIREMENT

This event is important to you, just as the previous events have been meaningful for your stepchild. You will want your family with you at such a milestone. Retirement is the ending of an era—a work era—but also the beginning of a new life for you. If you have a celebration, your stepchild will attend and be recognized as an important part of your life and achievements. This may be her turn to wear the flower and toast you. Once you are retired, you may have more time to spend with your stepfamily, although your stepchild may be an adult by this time and have her own life.

In your retirement, you may be able to help your stepchild out in spending time with your stepgrandchild or working on projects that you have some expertise in that your stepchild needs done in her home. How about planning a trip with your stepchild or continuing that annual event that you started years ago?

Build a Future Plan for You and Your Stepchild

Where do you see your relationship with your stepchild in five years? Where do you see that relationship in ten years? Sometimes we get so caught up in the day-to-day activities and routine that we don't get a chance to take a serious look at the future of our relationships. This is your chance to do just that. In this section, we will discuss the future of your relationship with your stepchild, and look at a future plan for both of you to work on together.

There are three basic sections to the future plan. The first section is reviewing the past history of your relationship with your stepchild. This will reveal conflicts or problems that you have experienced in the past. Both you and your stepchild have input in this section for two reasons. One, both of you get to compare the information that you write there. You might have indicated the same information; however, there is a chance that each of you listed different conflicts or problems that you have encountered in the past. That's great. This exercise is intended for you to learn new information, and it will help continue the bonding processes.

After listing any conflict from the past, the next step is to state how the situation was resolved—if it was. This is a valuable section because it may provide information on problem-solving successes that you have experienced in your relationship, but it also would reveal any unfinished business that suggests there is continued resolution to be done. For example, if your stepchild is still upset with you over an incident that may have occurred some time ago, you can now communicate. A good way to re-solve issues is to begin the discussion about them. If you were unaware that your stepchild felt this way, this is an excellent opportunity to work through the problem with him and open the avenues of communication toward a healthy and positive rela-tionship. Always make the effort to resolve leftover issues in your relationships. Resentment breeds unhappiness. You and your stepchild deserve more.

After completing the section about your past history, the plan moves into evaluating how your relationship feels to both of you. This is a brief narrative section that allows each of you to write down your feelings about one another. The key here is honesty, so it is important that you each be clear and concise about your feelings. This serves as a valuable tool for providing insight into your emotional vision and how you and your stepchild actually feel about your relationship. Sometimes this is information that we aren't readily aware of in our day-to-day interactions. If both of you indicate that your relationship is fine, that's great. How-ever, if either of you have a concern, this would be the place to note that and together offer information about how to resolve it.

Next in the plan is the opportunity to rate your relationship with your stepchild. You will both choose a rating of one through five, based on the categories given; one representing an unsat-isfactory relationship and five representing a fulfilling relation-ship. If, up to this point in the plan, there is little information from either of you revealing areas of improvement in your rela-tionship, this is a brief and to-the-point exercise that can help you both understand where the relationship is right now. This rating exercise provides a wonderful opportunity for discussion with your stepchild. If your stepchild chooses one through three, this would be a relatively strong indication that there is work that still needs to be done, and the next step in the plan provides a process for addressing just that.

Now both of you can list areas that still require work. These do not have to be major areas but can include smaller, sometimes frustrating issues that you may not have had the opportunity to address with each other. These issues may vary widely depending upon how old your stepchild is and if he is living out of your home and on his own. You may be thinking of issues right now that have concerned you about your stepchild and the right opportunity to talk about them has not yet presented itself—until you do this plan together. The plan can be used as a discussion and negotiation tool, plus it provides written documentation for you to retain and review periodically to check your progress on the issues that require continued work and monitoring.

Develop a plan to work through the problems that either you or your stepchild has listed. This step involves a simple contract of your joint commitment to the resolution of the issue. What you and your stepchild commit to should be something that you do intend to accomplish. First, list the issue that you both intend to work on. Second, list what you will do as the stepparent to help improve the area and resolve the issue. Third, the stepchild will list what she will do to help resolve the issue in her relationship with you. Then, indicate the ideal time when your stepchild and you would like to see the issue resolved. The date for resolution is important; neither one of you want the issue to continue forever, so it is clearly to your benefit to know when this issue will be clarified and resolved between you. Mark that date on the calendar with a big red star; ask your stepchild to do the same. You have just created another opportunity to work on a common project with your stepchild; one more step in the bonding adventure!

The final section of the plan is evaluating what both of you want your relationship to look like in the future. Each of you will have a comfort level that you want to reach in your relationship. If you have achieved this, great. If not, here is an opportunity for both of you to design your relationship. This is a grand opportunity to custom design your relationship now, and in the future. By writing down in the plan what you want this relationship to look like, you can show your stepchild what you want from this relationship. Your stepchild has the opportunity to do the same for you in this step of the plan. This step eliminates any guesswork about your relationship and what your expectations might be. After completing this plan, you will each have the information that you need to maintain a good, healthy, and positive relationship in the future—which could be the cornerstone for the continued success of your stepfamily.

FUTURE PLAN WITH YOUR STEPCHILD

Review your past history with your stepchild.

Problems we had in the past.   *How did we resolve them?*

_____   _____
_____   _____
_____   _____
_____   _____
_____   _____

Evaluate how your relationships feels to both of you now.

_____
_____
_____
_____

Rate your relationship with your stepchild on a scale of one to five.

1	2	3
unsatisfying	*still has conflict*	*good but needs work*
4	5	
comfortable	*fulfilling*	

List areas that still need work.

Stepparent   *Stepchild*

_____   _____
_____   _____
_____   _____
_____   _____

Develop a plan to work to problem solve each issue together.

Issue/Problem/Conflict _____
_____
_____

Stepparent will _____
_____
_____

to help resolve this issue.

Stepchild will _____
_____
_____

to help resolve this issue.

Goal: We would like to resolve this issue by (date) _____

Evaluate what each of you want your relationship to look like in the future.

Stepparent: I want my relationship with my stepchild, in the future, to _____
_____
_____

Stepchild: I want my relationship with my stepparent, in the future, to _____
_____
_____
_____

How You Know When You Are a Family

In a stepfamily, how do we know that we are now a family? What defines us as a family? While these questions may be answered differently in every family, there are some basic similarities between families. This exercise will help you determine, from those basic elements of the family, if your stepfamily has become a family.

Schedule a family meeting. Make it fun, with a cookout or a potluck dinner that everyone can participate in. Go around the room and have each family member discuss what they feel makes a family. Write down the ideas. It is likely that one or more of your family members will state the same qualities. That's good—you've got a theme going. Some of the ideas might be togetherness, caring for one another, looking out for each other, protecting one another, defending each other, attending church together, helping each other do things, or perhaps working together in a family business. Your list may include these ideas but also a variety of other thoughts about what makes a family. By the way, keep the list of ideas, as it will provide a marvelous keepsake in future years, as you and your partner fondly reminisce about your stepfamily—your created family.

Once everyone has had a separate turn stating their ideas of what makes a family, as a group, come up with a definition of your family. How would your family describe itself? This will be your list of what will indicate when you know that you have reached the status of family. This may be difficult at first, but here are some ideas to get you started:

- Caring about each other without thinking about it
- Responding to each other without having to think through your approach or worry about what you say and how you say it because you communicate with care
- Thinking of your stepchild as part of your family
- Talking to others about your stepchild as your own
- Looking around at everyone at the table with a genuine feeling of love—maybe even unconditional love

Hopefully, after applying some of the techniques from the book, combined with your hard work, you are now a family, a close-knit group that cares and respects each other. After reading this far and finishing the book. you have given you and your stepfamily the greatest gift of your efforts, creating harmony at home. You deserve a great deal of praise for your efforts. And, remember, never stop trying. Congratulations on a job well done.

Acknowledgments

Thanks to my parents, Lucille and Isadore, who love me very much, and to my siblings, Joanne, Peg, Tom, Paul, and Steven, who, even though we have lived miles apart at times in our lives, remain a source of comfort and support to me.

About the Author

Suzen J. Ziegahn, Ph.D., MBA, MA, is a clinical psychologist and writer specializing in stepfamily issues. She also has over fourteen years of experience in the administration of mental health services and has served as the CEO of a large mental health care system in the Midwest. Her shorter work has appeared in publications such as *Psychology Today*. She is a member of the American Psychological Association, and the stepmother of two children.